Ben-Tehillim

The Book of Psalms in English Blank Verse

Using the Verbal and Lineal Arrangements of the Original

Ben-Tehillim

The Book of Psalms in English Blank Verse
Using the Verbal and Lineal Arrangements of the Original

ISBN/EAN: 9783337020712

Printed in Europe, USA, Canada, Australia, Japan

Cover: Foto ©Lupo / pixelio.de

More available books at **www.hansebooks.com**

THE
BOOK OF PSALMS

IN ENGLISH BLANK VERSE

USING THE VERBAL AND LINEAL ARRANGEMENTS OF THE ORIGINAL

BY

BEN-TEHILLIM

EDINBURGH

ANDREW ELLIOT, 17 PRINCES STREET

1883

PREFACE.

MUCH attention has lately been given to the Book of Psalms, and a growing desire has been shown to chant the Authorized Version, as the Church of England chants the Prayer Book Version. Evidently, however, the two modes in which the Church of England uses the Prayer Book Version are both very faulty. In the reading of verses alternately by the minister and by the congregation, there is usually an unseemly haste to trip up each other's heels; while in the general chanting there are often ridiculous hop-step-and-jump movements, caused by the varying lengths of sentences. Therefore the thought presented itself, Is there no possibility of attaining a better plan? Let an attempt be made.

To chant a prose version is an absurdity: music being rhythmical, needs a rhythmical subject; as is moreover evidenced by the Hebrew Psalms having an arrangement of accents differing from that which is applied to the prose books of the Old Testament. Again, rhyme, while it is unlike the original, imposes on a faithful translator difficulties which are insurmountable; additions and omissions have to be made for the mere purposes of rhyme. Blank verse is therefore clearly the most suitable.

So then keeping faithfully to the original, the first thing was to ascertain the length and division of the lines. In most cases these are plain enough: yet there are many cases where much consideration was required; and after all it will be interesting to know what Biblical scholars will think about the accuracy of the arrangement here given. As a translation of line by line was aimed at, a great change from the arrangements of the Authorized Version was necessary; sometimes expanding, more frequently condensing, the sentences. The various Divine names have been retained as they occur, and also the repetition of pronouns where these are used emphatically. The order of words in the Hebrew has been carefully preserved as far as possible; uniformity has been attempted in the translation of words; the variations of tense in verbs have likewise been attended to. While it is hoped that in doing thus the English idiom has been sufficiently maintained, there is without doubt a clearer connection of ideas than can be traced in some parts of the Authorized Version.

Much satisfaction has been derived from finding that the original text shows no signs of corruptedness, which destructive critics are so fond of magnifying. On the contrary, the present translator has succeeded almost beyond his own expectation in making out what appears to himself an intelligible rendering. One or two passages remain obscure, not so much from their construction, as from the use of peculiar words: especially xxxv. 16; xlv 8, 13, 14; lxviii. 13, 27; lxxxvii. 7; cxxxix. 11; cl. 4.

The chief alterations made in translation are as follows: iv. 2; vii. 4, 11, 14; viii. 1, 8; x. 3, 4, 18; xvi. 2; xvii. 11; xix. 3; xxi. 12; xxii. 29-31; xxv. 14; xxvii. 13; xxxii. 9; xxxv. 13, 16; xliv. 12; xlv. 5, 8, 13, 14; xlix. 8, 9, 12, 14, 20; lvi. 7; lviii. 1, 2, 7-9; lix. 12; lxii. 11; lxiii. 10; lxviii. 13, 14, 16, 27, 30; lxxiii. 8, 11; lxxvii. 10; lxxxiv. 6; lxxxvi. 17; lxxxvii. 7; xc. 5, 9; cx. 6; cxix. 9, 57, 61, 67; cxxxix. 11, 16, 20; cxliv. 12-14; cl. 1.

The chief difficulties with the accents are—xvii. 13; xxviii. 9; xxxii. 5; xxxv. 7, 24; xxxvii. 23; xxxviii. 10; xlvi. 4; lix. 13; lx. 4, 6; lxii. 4; lxiv. 7; lxviii. 8, 10, 18, 19; lxix. 32; lxxi. 5; lxxii. 15; lxxiii. 8, 20; lxxvi. 5; lxxviii. 4; lxxix. 3; lxxxiv. 10; xci. 9; civ. 26; cv. 11; cx. 3; cxl. 11, 12; cxli. 8; cxlvii. 1.

If any competent scholars be inclined to look favourably on the present attempt, and think they can point out any improvements, either in translation or arrangement, their communications would be much esteemed; these may be addressed to my assumed name Ben-Tehillim, care of Mr. Andrew Elliot, publisher, 17 Princes Street, Edinburgh.

BEN-TEHILLIM.

December 15, 1882.

THE BOOK OF PSALMS.

PSALM I.

1.   O happy is the man
   Who hath not walked in counsel of the wicked,
   Nor in the way of sinners hath been standing,
   Nor in the seat of scorners hath been sitting:
2. But in Jehovah's law is his delight,
   And in that law he museth day and night.
3. He's like a tree set near the water-rills,
   One which will yield its fruit in season due,
       And fail not of its leaf:
   And all he takes in hand shall prosper well.
4.   Not so are wicked men;
   But are like chaff which wind shall drive away.
5. Therefore shall rise no wicked in the judgement,
   Nor sinners in assembly of the righteous.
6. Jehovah knows the way of righteous men,
   But way of wicked men shall perish quite.

PSALM II.

1. Wherefore did nations noisily consort,
   And will the peoples prate a vain desire?
2. Will stand be taken by the kings of earth,
   And were the rulers met conspiringly
   Against Jehovah and against his Christ?

3. Let us asunder break these bands of theirs,
   And cast away from us these cords of theirs.
4. He who is seated in the heavens will laugh;
   The Sovran Lord will be deriding them.
5. Then will he in his anger speak to them,
   And in his wrath will sorely trouble them.
6. Yet I have constituted mine own king
   On Zion which is mine own holy hill.
7.   I'll tell what is decreed;
   Jehovah said to me, My son art thou,
   'Tis I who have this day begotten thee.
8.   Ask thou from me,
   And I'll make nations be thy heritage,
   And thy possession reach the ends of earth.
9. Thou shalt o'errule them with an iron rod;
   Like potter's vessel thou shalt shiver them.
10. So now, ye kings, do ye be acting well;
    Do ye be warned, O judges of the earth:
11. Give service to Jehovah with due fear,
    Also do ye rejoice with tremblingness.
12.   Kiss ye the Son
    Lest he be angry, and ye lose the way.
    When in a little while his anger burns,
    Happy shall be all shelterers in him.

PSALM III.

1. Jehovah, O how many are my troublers!
   Many are rising up at me!
2.   Many are saying to my soul,
   There is no saving help for him in God.   Selah.
3. But thou, Jehovah, art a shield round me,
   My glory, and the raiser of my head.
4. Aloud unto Jehovah I will call,

    And me he'll answer from his holy hill.   Selah.
5. I did down-lay me, and would take my sleep;
        I have awaked again,
    Because Jehovah is upholding me.
6. I will not fear the myriads of folk
    Whom they have set against me round about.
7. Arise, Jehovah! save me, O my God!
    For thou hast smitten all my foes on cheek;
    The teeth of wicked men thou shattered hast.
8. Unto Jehovah is salvation due;
    Upon thy people may thy blessing be.   Selah.

PSALM IV.

1.   What time I call
    O answer me, my God of righteousness;
    In former strait thou didst enlarge for me;
    Show grace to me, and listen to my prayer.
2.   O sons of men,
    How long my glory trying to disgrace,
    Will ye love vainly, will ye seek a lie?   Selah.
3. But know ye that Jehovah puts apart
        The godly for himself;
    Jehovah will hear when I call to him.
4. Amid your raging, give not way to sin;
    Commune with your own heart upon your bed,
        And be ye still.   Selah.
5. Present ye offerings of righteousness,
    And to Jehovah turn your confidence.
6. Many are saying, Who will show us good?
        Do thou lift up on us
    The light, Jehovah, of thy countenance.
7. Thou hast put more of gladness in my heart
    Than when their corn and their new wine increased.

8. In peacefulness I will both lay me down
   And take my sleep;
For it is thou, Jehovah, thou alone,
Who wilt make me in confidence to sit.

PSALM V.

1. My saying give thou ear to, O Jehovah;
   Discern my musing plaint:
2. Be giving heed to my loud cry for help,
   O thou my King and God,
Because that unto thee will I appeal.
3. Jehovah, early shalt thou hear my voice;
At morn I'll set before thee and will watch.
4. For not a God of wicked tastes art thou;
   No ill can dwell with thee.
5. No boasters shall be setting themselves up
   To stand before thine eyes;
Thou hatest all who work ungodliness.
6. Thou wilt destroy the speakers of untruth;
   A man of bloodiness and of deceit
   Jehovah will abhor.
7. But I, through thine abounding mercy, I
   Will go into thy house;
I will bow down toward thy holy temple
   In reverent fear of thee.
8. Jehovah, lead me in thy righteousness
   Because of spying foes;
Do thou make straight before my face thy way.
9. For in their mouth there is no steadfastness;
   Inside they vicious are:
A sepulchre laid open is their throat;
Their tongue they will be making slippery.
10. Do thou decree them guilty, O great God;

Let them fall down through their own counsellings;
In their much trespass do thou drive them off
    As rebels against thee.
11. But glad shall be all shelterers in thee;
    They'll ever brightly sing,
    And thou wilt cover them;
Exult in thee shall lovers of thy name.
12. For thou, yea, thou wilt bless the righteous man,
    Jehovah, thou
Like buckler wilt with favour compass him.

PSALM VI.

1. JEHOVAH, not in anger check thou me;
Nor in thy hot wrath do thou chasten me.
2.   Show grace to me, Jehovah,
    For weakened down am I;
    Do thou heal me, Jehovah,
For sorely troubled have become my bones.
3. My soul is also troubled grievously;
And thou, Jehovah, O how long wilt be?
4. Return, Jehovah, extricate my soul;
O do thou save me for thy mercy's sake.
5. Because in death no memory is of thee;
In Sheol who can render thanks to thee?
6. I have been wearied with my constant sighs;
I every night will cause my bed to swim;
I with my tears will make my couch to melt.
7. Sunken through provocation is mine eye;
It is grown old through all my harassers.
8. Depart from me, ungodly doers all,
Because Jehovah hears my weeping voice.
9. Jehovah hath my supplication heard;
My humble prayer Jehovah will receive.

10. Ashamed and troubled grievously shall be
   Mine enemies each one;
   They shall retreat, shall be ashamed full quick.

PSALM VII.

1.   Jehovah, O my God,
   In thee I've shelter sought;
   O save me from all those pursuing me,
   And do thou rescue me,
2. Lest he be tearing, lionlike, my soul,
   Snatching when there is not a rescuer.
3. Jehovah, O my God, if I've done this,
   If there be real injustice in my hands;
4. If I have used my friendly neighbour ill,
   While yet I spare my reckless harasser;
5. Then let an enemy pursue my soul,
   And overtake, and tread to earth my life,
   And leave my glory lying in the dust.   Selah.
6. Be rising, O Jehovah, in thine anger!
   Be up at ragings of my harassers!
   And rouse for me the right thou hast ordained.
7. And let the peoples congregate round thee,
   And over them return thou to the height.
8. Jehovah will to nations give redress;
   Judge me, Jehovah, me
   As fits my righteousness and perfectness.
9. O that would cease the ill of wicked men;
   But stablish righteous man,
   And be a trier of the hearts and reins,
   Great God, thou righteous One.
10. My shield hath its dependence on great God,
    Who saveth them who be upright of heart.
11. Great God is verily a righteous judge,

Yet is a God indignant every day.
12. If man will not return, his sword he'll whet,
His bow is bent, and he will keep it strung;
13. And for him he hath ready shafts of death;
His arrows to be fiery he will make.
14. Behold! he pledgeth to ungodliness;
Hath conceived mischief, brought forth falsity.
15. A pit he digged, and he would bore it deep;
But he shall fall into the ditch he makes.
16. Back shall his mischief turn to his own head;
And on his pate his violence shall come down.
17. I'll thank Jehovah for his righteousness,
And tune the name Jehovah the Most High.

PSALM VIII.

1.   Jehovah, our great Lord,
How excellent thy name in all the earth!
Thou who dost put thy splendour on the heavens;
2. From mouth of children and of sucking babes
    Thou hast ordained strength
    Against thy harassers,
To quell the enemy and vengeful man.
3. When I behold thy heavens, thy fingers' work,
The moon and stars which thou hast marshalled forth,
4. What is frail man that thou rememberest him?
Or son of man that thou wilt visit him?
5. Wilt little lower him from angels' rank,
With honour and with glory wilt crown him?
6. Wilt make him rule the works of thine own hands?
All these thou hast put underneath his feet.
7. The sheep-flocks, and tame cattle, all of them,
Moreover the wild creatures of the field,
8. The bird of heaven, and fishes of the sea;

Himself a crosser of the paths of sea.
9.   Jehovah, our great Lord,
How excellent thy name in all the earth!

PSALM IX.

1. I'll give Jehovah thanks with all my heart;
   I will be telling all thy wondrous works.
2. I will be glad and will exult in thee;
   I will attune thy name, O thou Most High.
3. What time mine enemies be turned aback,
   Stumble shall they, and perish from thy face.
4. For thou hast wrought my right and my redress;
   Hast sat on throne adjudging righteously:
5. Hast rebuked nations, hast undone the bad;
   Their name hast blotted out for aye and aye.
6.   The enemy!
Complete perpetual desolations now!
   And cities thou didst pluck,
Perished is their remembrance, and themselves.
7. Whereas Jehovah evermore shall sit;
   He for the judgement hath prepared his throne.
8. And he, yea, he will judge the world aright;
   He will redress the peoples equally.
9. Jehovah is a safe height for the crushed;
   A safe height for the seasons of distress.
10. Confide in thee shall those who know thy name;
    For thou didst not forsake thy seekers, Lord.
11. Tune to Jehovah who in Zion sits;
    Show ye among the folks his constant deeds.
12. When tracing bloodshed he remembered them,
    Did not forget the outcry of the meek.
13.   Show grace to me, Jehovah;
    See what I suffer from those hating me!

O mine upraiser from the gates of death!
14. That so I may be telling all thy praise
    Within the gates of Zion's daughter fair;
    I may be joying in thy saving grace.
15. Sunk are the nations in the ditch they made;
    In that same net they hid, is caught their foot.
16. Known is Jehovah; judgment he hath wrought;
    In his own handwork snaring wicked man.
                                    Higgaion, Selah.
17. Back shall the wicked ones to Sheol turn;
    The nations all who are forgetting God.
18. But needy man shall ne'er be clean forgot;
    Nor shall the hope of meek ones perish quite.
19. Arise, Jehovah! let not man presume!
    Be nations judged in presence of thyself.
20. Do thou, Jehovah, put a fear in them;
    Let nations know that feeble men are they.   Selah.

PSALM X.

1. Why, O Jehovah, wilt thou stand far off?
   Wilt thou keep hid in seasons of distress?
2. In pride the wicked hotly hunts the meek;
   They will be caught in schemes which they contrive.
3. For wicked man did boast his soul's desire,
   And winning, he hath blessed, hath scorned Jehovah.
4. The wicked's haughty bearing will not seek:
   There is no God; 'tis wholly his own schemes.
5. His ways are self-sufficient at all times;
   High up thy judgements are above his view.
   All his harassers, he will puff at them.
6. He hath in heart said, I shall not be moved;
   To ages all shall be exempt from ill.
7.   With cursing teems his mouth,

And with deceit and fraud:
Under his tongue are mischief and untruth.
8. He'll sit in lurkings of the villages;
In secret spots he'll slay the innocent;
His eyes against the helpless closely hide.
9. He'll lurk in secret spot,
Like lion in his booth;
He'll lurk to catch the meek;
He'll catch the meek by dragging him in net.
10. He'll bruise, he will bow down
Till fall the helpless in his powerful grip.
11. He in his heart did say, God hath forgot,
Hath hid his face; he hath not seen at all.
12. Arise, Jehovah! God, lift up thy hand!
Forget not those who're meek.
13. Wherefore hath wicked man been scorning God?
Been saying in his heart, Thou wilt not seek?
14. But thou hast seen, for thou,
Yea, thou on mischief and despite wilt look
To punish with thy hand:
On thee the helpless one will leave himself;
The orphan, thou, yea, thou hast been his help.
15. Break thou the arm of wicked and ill man!
Thou'lt seek his wickedness till none be found.
16. Jehovah is the King for aye and aye:
Perished are heathen nations from his land.
17. Desire of meek folk thou, Jehovah, heardst;
Thou'lt firm their heart, wilt lend thy ready ear
18. For judging of the orphan and the crushed;
Till there shall be no more
Of tyrannizing by frail man of earth.

PSALM XI.

1. In Jehovah I shelter have taken;
   How then will ye say to my soul?
   Be shifting your mountain, O bird,
2.   For behold!
   Now the wicked are bending the bow;
   They have fitted their shaft on the string
   To be shooting from out of the dark
         At the hearts of uprightness.
3. When principles shall be made ruin,
   The righteous man, what hath he wrought?
4. Yet Jehovah's in his holy temple;
   Jehovah in heaven is throned.
         His eyes will be gazing,
   His eyelids be trying men's children.
5. Jehovah the righteous man trieth;
   But wicked and lover of violence,
         Them his soul hateth.
6. He will rain upon wicked men traps,
   Fire and brimstone, and furious tempest;
         The portion of their cup.
7. For righteous Jehovah will be;
   To righteousness he hath shown love;
   On the upright his face will be gazing.

PSALM XII.

1. Save thou, Jehovah, for the godly ceaseth;
   For faithful ones have failed from sons of men.
2. Vain is the talk of each man with his neighbour;
   With smoothing lip, and double heart they talk.
3. Jehovah will cut off all lips of smoothing;
   A tongue that will be talking of great things:

4. Who say, By our own tongues we will be mighty;
   Our lips are ours ; who is a lord o'er us?
5. The meek have been despoiled, the needy groaning,
   Now therefore I will rise, Jehovah saith;
   I'll put in safety him who pants for it.
6. The sayings of Jehovah are pure sayings,
   Like silver purged in earthen crucible,
        And sevenfold refined.
7. Thou, O Jehovah, wilt watch over them,
   Thou wilt safe-keep him from that race for ever.
8. On all sides will the wicked walk about
   When vileness towers among the sons of men.

PSALM XIII.

1. Till when, Jehovah, wilt forget me quite?
   Till when wilt thou keep hid thy face from me?
2. Till when shall I put counsels in my soul,
        With sorrow in my heart each day?
   Till when shall tower mine enemy o'er me?
3.   Be looking; answer me,
             Jehovah, O my God;
   Enlight mine eyes lest I should sleep in death;
4. Lest say mine enemy, I've mastered him.
   My troublers would rejoice if I were moved.
5. Yet I, I in thy mercy do confide;
   My heart rejoice would in thy saving grace.
6.   I will unto Jehovah sing
        When he hath kindly dealt to me.

PSALM XIV.

1. The fool saith in his heart, There is no God.
   They lead corrupt, abominable lives,
        There's no one doing good.

2. Jehovah from the heavens hath looked down
    Upon the sons of men,
 To see if there was any well inclined
    Inquiring after God.
3. The whole has turned; they're filthy through and through:
    There's no one doing good,
    There is not even one.
4. Have they no knowledge, all these wrongdoers,
 Eating my people, they have eaten bread,
  And on Jehovah have not called.
5.   There did they dread a dread!
 For the great God is with the righteous race.
6. The counsel of the meek man ye beshame
 Because Jehovah is his sheltering One.
7.   Who will from Zion give
    Safe help to Israel?
 When back Jehovah brings his captive folk
 Jacob shall joy, and Israel be glad.

PSALM XV.

1. JEHOVAH, who shall sojourn in thy tent?
 Who shall be dwelling on thy holy hill?
2. He who walks perfect, and acts righteously,
 And who speaks truthfully within his heart;
3. Who hath not carried tales upon his tongue;
 Who hath done nought of damage to his friend;
 Nor borne against his neighbour a reproach.
4. Contemned in whose eyes is a reprobate,
 While them that fear Jehovah he will prize:
 Though sworn to his own hurt, he will not change.
5. His coin he hath not put to usury;
 No bribe against the guiltless would he take.
 Whoso doth these things never shall be moved.

PSALM XVI.

1. Be watching over me, O God,
   For I am sheltering in thee.
2. I've to Jehovah said, Great Lord art thou;
   My goodness cannot be apart from thee
3. Toward those saints who are upon the earth,
   Those excellent who are my full delight.
4. Much sorrow they shall have who haste elsewhere;
   I will pour none of their blood-offerings,
   Nor will I take their names upon my lips.
5. Jehovah is my portioned share and cup:
   'Tis thou who art maintainer of my lot.
6. The lines are fallen to me in pleasant ways;
   Yea, mine hath been a goodly heritage.
7. I'll bless Jehovah, who hath counselled me;
   Yea, nightly have my reins been chastening me.
8. I've set Jehovah fronting me always,
   So from my right hand I shall not be moved.
9.   Therefore grew glad my heart;
         Joyful my tongue will be;
   Yea, and my flesh will dwell in confidence;
10. For thou wilt not forsake my soul to Sheol,
    Nor give thy godly one to see corruption.
11. Thou wilt cause me to know the path of life;
    Fulness of gladness near the face of thee;
    Pleasures in thy right hand surpassingly.

PSALM XVII.

1. Be hearing, O Jehovah, what is right;
   Do thou be giving heed to mine outcry;
   Do thou be giving ear unto my prayer,
   Which is from lips of no deceitfulness.
2. Forth from thy presence shall my judgement come,

Thine eyes will be beholding uprightly.
3. Thou prov'st my heart, hast visited by night;
   Hast purified me; nothing shalt thou find:
   I purpose that my mouth shall not transgress.
4. As to man's deeds, through word of thine own lips
   I've kept my watch on paths of daring sin,
5. So to maintain my goings in thy tracks
   As that my footsteps have not been removed.
6.   I earnestly have callèd thee,
       For thou wilt answer me, O God;
   Incline thine ear to me; O hear my speech.
7. Display thy mercies, saving sheltered ones
   From the uprising ones, by thy right hand.
8. Watch over me like apple of the eye;
   In shadow of thy wings thou wilt me hide,
9. From face of wicked men who've wasted me,
   My deadly foes who will encircle me,
10.   Wrapt up in their own fat,
    They with their mouth have spoken haughtily;
11. Our goings now have compassed him about;
    Their eyes they'll set down-looking to the earth.
12. He's like a lion longing for the prey,
    Or a young lion sitting secretly.
13. Arise, Jehovah! meet him face to face!
        Subdue him thoroughly!
    Set free my soul from wicked men, thy sword;
14. From mortal men, the hand of thee, Jehovah;
    From fleeting mortals, portioned in this life,
    And thy hid store thou fill'st their belly with;
        Sufficed are they with sons,
    And they will leave their plenty to their children.
15.   But I, yea, I in righteousness
          Shall gaze on face of thee;
        Shall be sufficed at waking-time
          With image of thyself.

PSALM XVIII.

1. I WILL love thee, Jehovah, thee my strength;
2. Jehovah is my crag, my fortalice,
    And my deliverer;
  My God, my rock in whom I shelter find,
  My shield, my horn of safety, my high place.
3. With praises due I'll to Jehovah call,
  And from mine enemies I shall be saved.
4. Had gathered over me the cords of death,
  And streams of Belial would be frighting me.
5. The cords of Sheol compassed me about;
  There were confronting me the snares of death.
6. In my distress I to Jehovah called,
  And I unto my God would cry for help:
  He from his temple listened to my voice,
    And my loud crying to himself
    Got entrance to the ears of him.
7. Then heaving and then shaking went the earth;
  And the foundations of the mountains quaked,
  And heaved themselves because he was in wrath.
8. There rose a smoke up in his angriness,
  Also a fire out from his mouth devoured:
  Enkindled coals were burning out from it.
9. And he would bow the heavens, and come down,
  And awful gloom was underneath his feet.
10. And he would ride on cherub, and would fly,
  And he would soar upon the wings of wind.
11. He would make darkness be his hiding-place;
  Around about him his pavilion was
  Darkness of waters, thick clouds of the skies.
12. From glare before him his thick clouds would pass,
    Hailstones and coals of fire.
13. Then would Jehovah thunder in the heavens,

And the Most High One would give out his voice,
Hailstones and coals of fire.
14. Then he sent arrows forth, and scattered them,
And lightnings plenty, and confounded them.
15. Then were the channels of the waters seen,
And the foundations of the world revealed,
Because of thy rebuking, O Jehovah,
The blowing of the spirit of thine anger.
16. He would send from on high, he would take me,
Would draw me out from waters manifold.
17. Would rescue me from my strong enemy,
And from my haters, when too much for me.
18. They would confront me in my bitter day,
Yet would Jehovah be a stay for me,
19. And would outbring me into ample room,
Would pull me through, for he delights in me.
20. Jehovah deals as fits my righteousness,
As fits my cleansèd hands he'll give to me.
21. For I have kept upon Jehovah's ways,
And have not wickedly forsook my God.
22. For all his judgements were in front of me;
His statutes I will not remove from me.
23. I also would be perfect toward him,
And keep myself from mine iniquity.
24. So will Jehovah meet my righteousness
And cleanness of my hands before his sight.
25. Unto the gracious, thou wilt gracious be;
To him who's perfect, thou wilt perfect be;
26. To him who's pure, thou wilt be purity;
But to the perverse, thou'lt be contrary.
27. For thou, yea, thou the humble folk wilt save,
But eyes of loftiness thou wilt bring low.
28. For thou, yea, thou wilt cause my lamp to shine,
Jehovah my God makes my darkness bright.

B

29. For I through thee shall overrun a troop,
    And by my God I'll overleap a wall.
30. The Almighty, perfect is the way of him;
    The saying of Jehovah is refined;
    He shieldeth all those sheltering in him.
31. For who can be a God beside Jehovah?
    And who is a strong rock except our God?
32. The Almighty One who girdeth me with force,
    And who will give perfection to my way:
33. Who makes my feet efficient like the hinds,
    And on my lofty heights will make me stand:
34. Who is the teacher of my hands for war,
    So that mine arms have bent a bow of brass.
35. And thou wilt give to me thy saving shield;
    And thy right hand will be supporting me;
    And thy humility will make me great.
36. Thou wilt enlarge my footsteps under me,
    And there's no slipping of mine ankle-bones.
37. I'll chase mine enemies, and overtake,
    And not return until they be consumed.
38. I shall so wound them that they cannot rise,
    They shall be falling underneath my feet.
39. Thou wilt gird me with forces for the war,
    Wilt bow down mine insurgents under me.
40. Mine enemies! thou'st given to me their neck;
    Also my haters! I will them suppress.
41. They'll cry for help, but there is none to save;
    Unto Jehovah, but he hears them not.
42. I'll beat them small as dust upon the wind;
    Like miring of the streets I'll empty them.
43. Thou wilt free me from strivings of the folk;
    Wilt set me for a head of Gentile tribes;
    A folk I have not known shall serve to me.
44. With hearing ear they'll hearken unto me;

The stranger sons will cringing come to me.
45.   The stranger sons shall fade,
And come in trembling from their fastnesses.
46. Jehovah lives, and blessèd be my rock,
And be exalted my salvation's God!
47. The Almighty One who doth avenge for me,
And will subject the nations under me.
48. He who doth free me from mine enemies;
Yea, from insurgents thou wilt me exalt;
From man of violence wilt rescue me.
49. Therefore I'll thank thee 'mid the nations, Lord,
And to thy name I will be tuning psalms:
50. Author of great salvations to his king,
Of mercy to his own Anointed One,
To David, and his seed for evermore.

PSALM XIX.

1. THE heavens declare the gloriousness of God;
And his hands'-work the firmament displays.
2. Day unto day is issuing discourse;
And night to night is making knowledge plain.
3. There's no discoursing, and there are no words;
Ne'er hath been heard their voice.
4. O'er all the earth has gone abroad their line,
And to the world's end their argument.
He for the sun hath placed a tent in them,
5. Who like a bridegroom from his chamber comes,
Rejoicing hero-like to run the path.
6. From end of heavens will his coming be,
And his high circuit to the ends of them;
And there is nothing hidden from his heat.
7. The doctrine of Jehovah perfect is,
Restablishing the soul;

   The witness of Jehovah faithful is,
     To make the simple wise.
 8. The precepts of Jehovah are upright,
     Engladdening the heart;
   Commandment of Jehovah is most pure,
     Enlightening the eyes.
 9. The fearing of Jehovah cleansing is,
     Enduring evermore;
   The judgements of Jehovah truthful are,
     And righteous every one.
10. Desirable are they far more than gold,
     Yea, more than much fine gold;
   And sweeter far be they than honey is,
     Or droppings from the combs.
11. Likewise thy servant hath been warned by them,
   In keeping them there is a great reward.
12. His thoughtless errors who can understand?
   From secret sins keep thou me innocent:
13. Also from proud ones hold thy servant back;
   Let them not rule me; then shall I be whole,
   And innocent from greatly trespassing.
14. Accepted be the sayings of my mouth,
   The musings of my heart in sight of thee,
   Jehovah, my strong rock, my ransomer.

PSALM XX.

 1. Jehovah answer thee in troublous day!
   The name of Jacob's God safe-set thee high!
 2. May he send forth thy help from sanctuary,
   Also from Zion be sustaining thee!
 3. May he remember all thine offerings,
   And thy burnt-sacrifice may he accept!   Selah.
 4. May he give thee according to thy heart,

And all thy counselling may he fulfil!
5. We will sing brightly in thy victory,
And in our God's name bear our banners up.
O may Jehovah grant all thy requests!
6.   Now I am sure of this,
Jehovah saveth his Anointed One;
He will him answer from his holy heavens
With saving mightiness of his right hand.
7. Some in their chariots, some in horses boast,
      But we, we verily
In naming of Jehovah our own God.
8. They, they have bowed, and they are fallen down;
But we, we verily have risen up,
      And can present ourselves.
9.   Jehovah, do thou save!
The King will answer us
In day when we do call.

PSALM XXI.

1. JEHOVAH, in thy strength the king is glad;
In thy salvation O how much he'll joy!
2. His heart's desire thou hast been granting him;
His lips' petition thou hast not withheld.   Selah.
3. For thou confrontest him with blessings good;
Wilt set upon his head a crown of gold.
4. Life he did ask from thee; thou gavest him
Continuance of days for evermore.
5. Great is his glory through thy saving grace;
Honour and majesty thou'lt fit on him.
6. For thou wilt make him blessings till the end,
Wilt cherish him in gladness with thy face.
7. Because the king doth in Jehovah trust,
Through grace of the Most High he shan't be moved.

8. Thy hand will find out all thine enemies;
   Thy right hand will find out those hating thee.
9. Thou wilt make them like to a fiery kiln,
       What time thou shalt appear;
   Jehovah will in anger swallow them,
       And fire shall eat them up.
10. Their fruit from off the earth thou wilt destroy;
    Also their seed from 'mid the sons of men.
11. For they intended evil against thee;
    They planned a scheme, yet they shall not succeed.
12. Because that thou wilt make of them a butt;
    From off thy strings wilt aim against their face.
13. Exalt thyself, Jehovah, in thy strength!
    We will be singing, tuning of thy might.

PSALM XXII.

1. My God, my God, O why forsak'st thou me?
       Far from my saving help,
       The matters of my roar.
2. O mine own God, I will call out by day,
       And thou wilt not reply;
   Also by night, and I have no repose.
3.   But thou'rt the Holy One
   Inhabiting the praise of Israel.
4. In thee our forefathers did put their trust;
   They trusted, and thou wouldst deliver them.
5. To thee they did cry out, and got escape;
   In thee they trusted, and were not beshamed.
6. But I, I am a worm, and not a man;
   Reviled by men, and scouted by the people.
7. All they who see me will be mocking me;
   They will push out the lip, will shake the head:
8. Leave to Jehovah; he'll deliver him;

He'll rescue him, since he delights in him.
9. But it was thou didst draw me from the womb,
Making me trustful on my mother's breast :
10. On thee have I been cast from hour of birth;
Even from my mother's womb my God art thou.
11.   Be thou not far from me
   When trouble is come near,
   When there is none to help.
12. There have been compassing me many bulls ;
Strong ones of Bashan have beset me round:
13. They have wide opened against me their mouth,
A lion that doth ravin and doth roar.
14. Like unto waters I have been poured out,
And loosed asunder have been all my bones :
  My heart has been like very wax
  Down-melted in the midst of me.
15. Dry as a potsherd has become my strength,
Also my tongue is clinging to my jaws ;
And to the dust of death thou'lt bring me down.
16. For there have been encompassing me dogs ;
A crowd of evil men encircles me ;
They have been piercing both my hands and feet.
17. I may be taking count of all my bones ;
While these men, they will look, will stare at me.
18. They'll portion out my garments for themselves,
And on my vesture they will cast a lot.
19. But thou, Jehovah, be not thou far off !
My Strengthener, O to my help make haste !
20. O do thou rescue from the sword my soul !
Out from the hand of dog my lonely life !
21. O do thou save me from the lion's mouth !
And from the wild bulls' horns thou'st answered me.
22. I will declare thy name unto my kin ;
Amid the assembly I'll be praising thee.

23. O fearers of Jehovah, praise ye him!
    All ye the seed of Jacob, honour him!
    And be afraid of him, all Israel's seed!
24. For he hath not despised, nor hath abhorred
        The suffering of the meek,
    Nor did he keep his presence hid from him,
    But when he cried to him for help, he heard.
25. From thee my praise is in the great assembly;
    My vows I'll pay before his fearing ones.
26. Meek ones shall eat, and shall be satisfied;
    The seekers of Jehovah shall praise him;
        Your hearts shall live for aye.
27. Remember and return unto Jehovah
        Shall all the ends of earth;
    And down shall bow in worship before thee
        All nations' families.
28. For with Jehovah is the kingly reign,
        And he o'er nations rules.
29. Have eaten and in worship will bow down
        All fat ones of the earth.
        Before his face shall bend
        All goers down to dust,
        And each unquickened soul.
30.   A seed shall serve to him;
    It shall be counted for the Lord's own race.
31. They coming shall display his righteousness
    Unto a people born through what he did.

PSALM XXIII.

1. JEHOVAH is my shepherd; I'll not want.
2. In pastures green he'll cause me to lie down;
    Beside still waters he will nurture me.
3.   My soul he will restore;

He'll lead me in the tracks of righteousness
    Even for his name's sake.
4. Yea, though I walk through valley of death-shade
I'll fear no evil, for thou art with me;
This rod of thine, and helpful staff of thine,
    They, they shall comfort me.
5. Thou wilt prepare for me a table spread
    In presence of my foes;
Thou hast anointed copiously my head;
    My cup doth overflow.
6. Surely will good and mercy follow me
    Through all my days of life;
And I shall dwell within Jehovah's house
    To a long stretch of days.

PSALM XXIV.

1. To Jehovah the earth and its fulness,
The world and its dwellers belong.
2. For 'tis he who o'er ocean did found it,
And he o'er the streams keeps it firm.
3. Who shall climb to the mount of Jehovah,
Or stand within his holy place?
4. He of innocent hands and pure bosom,
Who lent not his soul unto folly,
Nor granted an oath in deceit.
5. He shall get from Jehovah a blessing,
And rightness from his Saviour God.
6.   Such the race of his seekers,
Inquiring thy presence, the Jacob.   Selah.
7. Lift up, O ye gates, your heads high!
And be lifted, ye doors everlasting!
And the glorious King shall come in.
8. But who is this glorious King?

'Tis Jehovah the strong and the mighty,
Jehovah the mighty in war.
9. Lift up, O ye gates, your heads high!
And uplift, O ye doors everlasting!
And the glorious King shall come in.
10. Who may he be, this glorious King?
Jehovah of hosts,
Even he is the glorious King. Selah.

PSALM XXV.

1. To thee, Jehovah, I will lift my soul.
2. My God, in thee have I put confidence;
O let me not be shamed;
Let not mine enemies exult o'er me.
3. Yea, none who wait on thee shall be ashamed;
Ashamed be those who reckless traitors are.
4. Thy ways, Jehovah, do thou make me know;
Thy very paths do thou be teaching me.
5. Do thou cause me to tread within thy truth,
And be thou teaching me:
For thou the God of my salvation art;
On thee have I been waiting all the day.
6. Remember thy compassions, O Jehovah,
Also thy mercies past,
For from of old are they.
7. Sins of my youthhood, and my trespasses
Do thou remember not.
As fits thy grace remember me do thou,
For sake of thine own goodness, O Jehovah.
8. Both good and upright hath Jehovah been;
Therefore will he point sinners in the way.
9. He'll make the humble ones in judgement tread,
And he will teach the humble ones his way.

10. Jehovah's paths all mercy are and truth
    To them who keep his covenant and laws,
11. Even for sake of thine own name, Jehovah;
    And thou hast pardoned mine iniquity
        Although it was so great.
12. Whatever man there be who fears Jehovah,
    Him will he point in way that he should choose.
13. The soul of him in welfare shall be lodged;
    The seed of him, too, shall possess the earth.
14. Jehovah's secret's for those fearing him;
    His covenant also is to make them know.
15. Mine eyes are constantly toward Jehovah,
    That he, yea, he may clear from net my feet.
16. Turn thou toward me, and show grace to me,
    Because a lonely suffering one am I.
17. The troubles of my heart have been enlarged;
    O from mine anguishments bring thou me out.
18. See mine affliction and my misery,
    And be thou taking all my sins away.
19. See how mine enemies are multiplied,
    And with what vicious hate they've hated me.
20. Be watching o'er my soul, and rescue me;
    Beshame not me, a shelterer in thee.
21. Let perfect rightness be preserving me
        Because I wait on thee.
22. Great God, be thou redeeming Israel
        From all that troubles him.

PSALM XXVI.

1.   JUDGE me, O thou Jehovah;
    For I in mine integrity have walked:
    Since in Jehovah I've put confidence
        I shall not slide.

2. Try me, Jehovah, and make proof of me;
　　Be thou refining both my reins and heart.
3. For thine own mercy is before mine eyes,
　　And I have practised walking in thy truth.
4. I have not sat with mortals of no worth;
　　And with dissemblers I will not go in.
5. I've hated the assembly of ill men,
　　And with the wicked ones I will not sit.
6. But I will wash in innocence my hands,
　　And will be compassing thine altar, Lord,
7. To publish with a voice of thanksgiving,
　　And make recount of all thy wondrous works.
8. Jehovah, I have loved thy house's seat,
　　And place of dwelling of thy gloriousness.
9. O gather not with sinful men my soul,
　　Neither with men of bloodiness my life;
10. Those who have in their hands a bad device,
　　And whose right hand is full of bribery.
11. But I in mine integrity will walk;
　　Do thou redeem me, and show grace to me.
12. My foot hath stood upon an even place;
　　In congregations I will bless Jehovah.

PSALM XXVII.

1. Jehovah's my light and salvation;
　　　　Whom then should I fear?
　Jehovah's the strength of my being;
　　　　Whom then shall I dread?
2. When nigh against me came ill-doers
　　　　To eat up my flesh,
　My troublers and enemies, they then
　　　　Did stumble and fall.

3. Though armies against me were camping,
           My heart should not fear;
   Though war were arising against me,
   In this I would confident be.
4. One thing I have asked from Jehovah,
           And that will I seek;
   May I sit in the house of Jehovah
           All days of my life,
   To gaze on delights of Jehovah,
   And fully inquire in his temple.
5. For close he'll hide me in pavilion
           Through each evil day;
   He'll secrete me within his tent's secret;
   On rock he will raise me up high.
6. And now shall my head be exalted
   Above these mine enemies round me;
   And I in his tent will be offering
           Oblations of joy;
   I'll sing and attune to Jehovah.
7. Hear, Jehovah! aloud I will call;
   And show grace to me, and give me answer.
8.   To thee said my heart,
           O seek ye my face;
   Thy face, O Jehovah, I'll seek.
9. Be not hiding thy presence from me;
   Dismiss not in anger thy servant;
           My help thou hast been:
   O leave me not, neither forsake me,
           My Saviour God.
10. When my father and mother forsake me
    Jehovah will gather me up.
11. O point me, Jehovah, thy way,
    And lead me in path of directness
            Because of my spiers.

12. Give me not to the will of my troublers;
    Though rose at me men of false witness,
        And violence spake,
13.   Yet I have had faith
    To see the good things of Jehovah;
        In land of the living.
14.   Wait thou for Jehovah;
    Be firm, and he'll strengthen thy heart;
        So wait thou for Jehovah.

PSALM XXVIII.

1. Unto thee, O Jehovah, I'll call;
   O my rock, be not heedless from me;
   Lest if thou shouldst be silent from me
   I be classed with down-goers to pit.
2. Be thou hearing my suppliant voice,
        When I cry for thy help;
        When I lift up my hands
   Toward oracle holy of thine.
3. Draw me not with the wicked away,
        Nor with actors ungodly;
   Those who speak kindly words with their friends
        While there's harm in their hearts.
4. Give to them as befits their own act,
   And as fits the ill course of their deeds;
   Like the work of their hands give to them;
   Render back their own treatment to them.
5.   Since they will not give heed
        To the acts of Jehovah
        And the work of his hands,
   He will wreck them, and not build them up.
6.   O blest be Jehovah!
   For he heareth my suppliant voice.

7. O Jehovah, my strength and my shield!
   In him trusteth my heart, and I'm helped:
   So my heart shall exult,
   And with song I will render him thanks.
8. O Jehovah the strength of his folk!
   And a full saving strength
   His Anointed One is.
9. Be thou saving this people of thine!
   And be blessing thine own heritage!
   And be shepherding, carrying them
   Through the ages to come.

PSALM XXIX.

1. ASCRIBE to Jehovah, ye sons of the mighty,
   Ascribe to Jehovah both glory and strength!
2. Ascribe to Jehovah his name's proper glory;
   O bow yourselves down to Jehovah
   In beauty of holiness.
3. The voice of Jehovah is out on the waters;
   The glorious Almighty hath thundered:
   Jehovah is over the manifold waters.
4. The voice of Jehovah in powerfulness;
   The voice of Jehovah in majesty.
5. The voice of Jehovah is breaking the cedars;
   Jehovah will shatter in pieces
   The cedars of Lebanon.
6. He also will make them to skip like a calf;
   Both Lebanon mountain and Sirion
   Like as a son of wild bulls.
7.   The voice of Jehovah
   Is dashing forth flashes of fire.
8. The voice of Jehovah will quiver the desert;
   Jehovah will quiver the desert of Kadesh.

9. The voice of Jehovah will make the hinds calve,
   And will strip the woods bare:
   While in his own temple
   The whole of it telleth of glory.
10. Jehovah in time of the deluge did sit;
   And Jehovah will sit as the King evermore.
11. Jehovah will strength to his people bestow;
   And Jehovah will bless
   His own people with peace.

PSALM XXX.

1. JEHOVAH, I will be extolling thee,
   For thou hast drawn me up,
   And not made glad mine enemies at me.
2. Jehovah, O my God,
   I cried to thee for help,
   And thou'lt be healing me.
3. Jehovah, thou
   Hast caused my soul from Sheol to come up,
   Hast quickened me from going down to pit.
4. Attune unto Jehovah, ye his saints;
   Give thanks in memory of his holiness.
5. Though but a moment in his anger,
   Life comes fully with his favour;
   Though at eve may linger weeping,
   Yet at morn shall come bright singing.
6. And I, I said in my prosperity,
   I never shall be moved;
7. Jehovah, in thy favour
   Thou wast establishing my mountain strong;
   Thou hast kept hid thy face,
   I have been troubled sore.
8. Unto thyself, Jehovah, I will call;
   And to Jehovah I will supplicate.

9.   What profit is there in my blood,
       In my descending to the ditch?
       Shall dust be giving thanks to thee?
       Shall it be showing forth thy truth?
10. Hear, O Jehovah, and show grace to me;
      Jehovah, O be thou a help to me.
11. Thou'st turned my wailing to a dance for me;
        Hast laid my sackcloth loose,
        And girded me with gladness.
12. That so may tongue be tuning psalms of thee,
        And not be still:
        Jehovah, O my God,
        I'll ever give thee thanks.

PSALM XXXI.

1. In thee, Jehovah, shelter I have sought;
   O let me not be put to shame for aye;
   In thine own righteousness give me escape.
2. Be thou inclining unto me thine ear;
   With speediness O do thou rescue me.
   Be thou to me for a stronghold of rock,
   For a well-fencèd house for saving me.
3. Because my crag and fortalice art thou;
       And for thine own name's sake
   Thou wilt both lead me, and wilt nurture me.
4. Thou'lt bring me out from net they've hid for me,
       Because thou art my strength.
5. Into thy hand I will commit my spirit;
       Thou hast redeemed me,
       Jehovah, God of truth.
6. I've hated those observing worthless shams;
   But I, toward Jehovah I've put trust.
7. I would rejoice and gladden in thy mercy,

      For thou didst look on mine afflicted state,
      Thou didst well know the troubles of my soul;
8. And didst not shut me in an enemy's hand;
      Thou gav'st my feet a stand in ample room.
9. Show grace to me, Jehovah, in my strait:
      Sunken through provocation is mine eye,
          My soul, my belly too.
10. For wasting off in sorrow is my life,
        Also my years in sighing;
    My strength is weak through mine iniquity,
        Also my bones have sunk.
11. Through all my troublers I've been a reproach,
        And to my neighbours greatly:
    Also a dread to mine acquaintances:
          They seeing me in street
          Did flit away from me.
12. I am forgot like dead man out of mind;
    I have been like a vessel perishing.
13. For I have heard the slanders manifold,
        Terror on every side;
    In their combined consulting against me
    To take away my life they have resolved.
14.   But as for me,
    I upon thee, Jehovah, have put trust;
    I have been saying, Mine own God art thou.
15.   In thy hand are my times;
    O rescue me from hand of enemies
        And from my persecutors.
16. Shine thou upon thy servant with thy face;
    O in thy mercy be thou saving me.
17. Jehovah, let me not be put to shame,
        For I have callèd thee:
        In shame shall wicked men
        To Sheol-silence go.

18. Struck dumb shall be the lips of falsity
    Which speak against a righteous man hard things
        With proudness and contempt.
19.   How great thy goodness is
    Which thou hast stored up for those fearing thee;
    Hast wrought out for those sheltering with thee
        In front of sons of men!
20. Thou wilt secrete them in thy secret presence
        From artful plots of man:
        Wilt hide them in pavilion
        Close from the strife of tongues.
21.   Blest may Jehovah be!
    For wondrous mercy he hath shown to me
        In city fortified.
22. Though I, yea, I had said in frighted haste,
    Cut off have I been from before thine eyes,
    Yet truly thou hast heard my suppliant voice
        When I cried for thy help.
23. Love ye Jehovah, all his sainted ones!
    The faithful ones Jehovah doth preserve;
    But he repayeth even plenteously
        To him who acts in pride.
24. Be firm, and he will give you strength of heart,
    All ye who to Jehovah look with hope.

PSALM XXXII.

1. HAPPY is he whose trespass is forgiven,
        Whose sin is covered up.
2.   O happy man to whom
    Jehovah will not charge iniquity,
    And in whose spirit is no guilefulness.
3. When I kept heedless, then my bones wore down
    Amid my roaring throughout all the day.

4. Since both by day and night
   Would weigh on me thine hand;
   Changed hath my moisture been
   Into a summer drought.   Selah.
5. My sin I would acknowledge unto thee,
   And mine iniquity I covered not.
   I said that to Jehovah
   I'll make confession of my trespasses;
   And thou, yea, thou forgavest
   My sin's iniquity.   Selah.
6. Because of this
   Each godly one shall make his prayer to thee
   At finding-time:
   Surely when many waters overflow
   Nigh him they shall not reach.
7. Thou art a hiding-place for me;
   From trouble thou wilt me preserve;
   With songs of glad escape
   Thou wilt encompass me.   Selah.
8. I will instruct thee, and be pointing thee
   In way which thou shalt go;
   I will give counsel, with mine eye on thee.
9. Be ye not like the horse or like the mule
   Which do not understand:
   With bit and bridle must their mouth be held
   When they're not near to thee.
10. Many sore pains befall the wicked man;
    But whoso in Jehovah putteth trust,
    Mercy shall compass him about.
11. Glad in Jehovah may you be,
    Also rejoice, ye righteous ones!
    And brightly sing, all ye upright of heart.

PSALM XXXIII.

1. Sing brightly, O ye righteous, in Jehovah;
   To upright ones a comely thing is praise.
2. Give thanks unto Jehovah with the harp;
   With ten-stringed psaltery tune ye to him.
3. Be singing unto him a new-made song;
   Be playing skilfully with joyful shout.
4. Because upright hath been Jehovah's word,
   And all his works have been in faithfulness.
5. He loveth righteousness and judgement just;
   With mercy of Jehovah earth is filled.
6. 'Twas by Jehovah's word the heavens were made,
   And by the breath of his mouth all their host.
7. Amassing like a heap the watery sea;
   Putting in storehouses the surging depths.
8. Afraid shall all the earth be of Jehovah;
   From him shall shrink all dwellers of the world.
9. For he, yea, he did say, and it would be;
   Yea, he commanded, and it firm shall stand.
10. Jehovah foiled the counsel nations took;
    He made the projects of the peoples nought.
11. The counsel of Jehovah stands for aye;
    The projects of his heart to every age.
12.   Happy that nation is,
    Even it which hath Jehovah for its God;
    The folk he chose for his own heritage.
13. From out of heaven did Jehovah look;
    He hath seen all the children of mankind:
14. From his established seat he hath looked forth
    At all who are the dwellers upon earth;
15. He fashioning alike the hearts of them,
    He understanding all the works of them.
16. No king is saved by an abundant force.

No champion rescued by abundant strength.
17. Untrusty is the horse for saving help,
Nor through abundant force gives he escape.
18.   Behold!
Jehovah's eye is on those fearing him,
On them who are the hopers for his mercy,
19. To be delivering from death their soul,
And to keep them alive in famine-time.
20. Our soul hath fondly waited for Jehovah;
Our helper and our shielder he will be.
21. For 'tis through him that glad shall be our heart,
For in his holy name have we put trust.
22. Thy mercy, O Jehovah, be on us
According as we've looked to thee in hope.

PSALM XXXIV.

1. O, I WILL bless Jehovah at all times;
Continually his praises in my mouth.
2. My soul shall in Jehovah make its boast;
The humble ones shall hear, and will be glad.
3. O magnify Jehovah, ye with me;
And we together will extol his name.
4. I sought Jehovah, and he answered me,
And out from all my fears he rescued me.
5. Those looking unto him were brightened up;
Their faces too, let them not be dismayed.
6. This poor man callèd, and Jehovah heard,
And from all his distresses savèd him.
7. The angel of Jehovah doth encamp
Around his fearers, and will pull them through.
8. Taste ye and see that good Jehovah is;
Happy the man who sheltereth in him.
9. O fear Jehovah, ye his holy ones,

For nought is lacking to those fearing him.
10. The lions young may lean and hungry be;
    But they who seek Jehovah
    Shall not lack any good.
11. O come, ye children, hearken unto me;
    Jehovah's fear I will be teaching you.
12. Who is the man that hath delight in life,
    That loveth days wherein he may see good?
13. Be thou preserving thine own tongue from ill,
    Also thy lips from speaking in deceit.
14. Depart from ill, and be thou doing good;
    Seek thou for peace, and be pursuing it.
15. Jehovah's eyes are toward righteous folk,
    Also his ears toward their cry for help.
16. Jehovah's face will be on ill-doers
    To cut from off the earth their memory.
17. Those who were crying out, Jehovah heard,
    And from all their distresses rescued them.
18. Near is Jehovah to the broken hearts,
    And them of bruisèd spirit he will save.
19. Though many evils reach a righteous man,
    From all these will Jehovah rescue him;
20. He keeping watchfully his every bone,
    Not even one of them shall have been broke.
21. Evil will put to death a wicked man,
    And haters of a righteous man have guilt.
22. Jehovah doth redeem his servants' souls;
    No guilt have any shelterers in him.

PSALM XXXV.

1. CHIDE thou, Jehovah, them who chide at me;
    Fight them who fight at me.
2. Do thou take hold of buckler and of shield

               And rise in help of me.
3.   Also draw out the spear
    And stop the way of my pursuing foes.
        Say thou unto my soul,
        Thy Saviour am I.
4. They shall be put to shame and to disgrace,
        The seekers of my soul;
    They shall be turnèd backward and dismayed,
        Devisers of my hurt.
5. They shall be like as chaff before the wind,
    And angel of Jehovah thrusting out:
6. Their way shall be both dark and slippery,
    And angel of Jehovah chasing them.
7. For without cause they hid for me their net;
    They without cause dug ditches for my soul.
8. There shall come on him ruin unawares;
    And net which he had hid shall catch himself;
        With ruin he shall fall in it.
9. But my soul shall be joying in Jehovah,
    Shall be rejoicing in his saving grace.
10. All of my bones shall be exclaiming thus,
    Who, O Jehovah, can be like to thee?
    Ridding the weak one from his stronger foe,
    The weak and needy from his plunderer.
11. Rise up will witnesses of violence;
    Things which I know not, they will ask of me;
12. They will repay me ill instead of good,
        Bereaving to my soul.
13.   But as for me,
    When they were sick, I did put sackcloth on,
    I did afflict with abstinence my soul,
    Also my prayer would on my breast return.
14. As to a friend, or brother, I behaved;
    As o'er lost mother, mourning I bowed down.
15. Yet when I limp, they gladden and consort;

Abjects have been consorted against me,
   And I was not aware;
They have been rending, and have not been still.
16. Among profaning scoffers mingled up,
   A-gnashing against me the teeth of them.
17. O Sovran Lord, how long wilt thou look on?
   Bring back my soul out from their ruinings,
   Out from the lions young my lonely life.
18. I will thank thee in an assembly great;
   Amid a mighty people I'll praise thee.
19. Let not my wrongful foes be glad at me;
   Let not my causeless haters wink the eye.
20. For it is not of peace that they will speak;
   But they against the quiet ones of earth
   Will matters of deceitfulness devise:
21. And they will widen against me their mouth,
      They've said, Aha, aha!
      Our very eye hath seen.
22. Jehovah, thou hast seen; not heedless be!
   Do thou, great Lord, be not afar from me.
23. Arouse thee, and wake up to judge my right,
   My God and Sovran Lord, to plead my cause!
24. Judge me in thine own righteousness, Jehovah,
   And let them not be glad at me, my God.
25. Let them not say in heart, Aha, our wish!
   Let them not say, We have quite swallowed him.
26. Those shall be shamed together and dismayed
      Who gladden at my hurt;
   Those shall be clothed with shame and with disgrace
      Who greatly swell at me.
27. Those shall be singing brightly and be glad
      Who love my righteous cause;
      And they shall say always,
      Great shall Jehovah be,
Who takes delight in his own servant's peace.

28. So shall my tongue rehearse thy righteousness;
All the day long it shall be praising thee.

PSALM XXXVI.

1. TRANSGRESSION telleth of the wicked man
   Unto my inmost heart,
   There is not any dread of the great God
   Before the eyes of him.
2. For he hath smoothed to it in his own eyes
   Till his iniquity be ha. eful found.
3. His words of mouth a. godlessness and guile;
   He ceaseth to act wisely, to do good.
4. Ungodliness he'll think upon his bed;
   He'll take his stand upon a way not good:
   Evil he will not loathe.
5. Jehovah, in the heavens thy mercy is;
   Thy faithfulness doth reach unto the skies;
6. Thy righteousness is like the hills of God;
   Thy judgements an unmeasurable deep:
   Both man and beast wilt thou, Jehovah, save.
7. How precious is thy mercy, O great God!
   Also the sons of men
   In shadow of thy wings will shelter take.
8. They shall be flushed from fatness of thy house;
   Thy stream of pleasures thou wilt make them drink.
9. Because with thee remains the fount of life;
   Through thine own light shall we be seeing light.
10. Draw out thy mercy to those knowing thee,
    Also thy righteousness to upright hearts.
11. Let not the foot of pride intrude on me,
    Nor hand of wicked men be ousting me.
12. There did ungodly doers have a fall;
    They are struck down, so that they cannot rise.

PSALM XXXVII.

1. Fret not thyself because of evil men,
   Envy not those who do what is unjust.
2. For like the grass they quickly shall be mown;
   And like green herbage they shall fade away.
3. Trust in Jehovah, and be doing good;
   Inhabit earth, and feed thou faithfully.
4. Also do thou delight thee in Jehovah,
   And he will give thee what thy heart shall ask.
5. Roll thou upon Jehovah's care thy way,
   And trust on him, and he, yea, he will work;
6. Forth-bringing like the light thy righteousness,
   Also thy judgement like the full noonday.
7. Calm to Jehovah, stay thyself to him;
   Fret not at one who prospereth his way,
   Or at another working evil plots.
8. Cease thou from anger, and abandon wrath;
   Be not thou fretting only to do ill.
9. For evil-doers are to be cut off;
   But waiters on Jehovah, even they,
         They shall possess the earth.
10. And very soon the wicked man is not;
    And thou hast carefully observed his place,
         And there is nought of him.
11. Whereas the meek ones shall possess the earth,
    And shall delight themselves in plenteous peace.
12. The wicked plotteth at the righteous man,
    And will be gnashing against him his teeth;
13. The Sovran Lord will surely laugh at him,
    Because he seeth that his day will come.
14. A sword the wicked have been drawing out,
         And they have bent their bow
    To overthrow the weak and needy one,

To slaughter them who be upright of way.
15. Their sword shall enter into their own heart,
Also the bows of them shall broken be.
16. Better is little to a righteous man
Than is the stir of many wicked men.
17. For arms of wicked men shall broken be,
But righteous men Jehovah doth hold up.
18. Jehovah knows the days of perfect men,
And their inheritance shall be for aye.
19. They shall not be in shame through evil time;
In days of dearth they shall be satisfied.
20. But wicked men, they shall be perishing;
Jehovah's enemies like fat of lambs
Have wasted off; in smoke have wasted off.
21. The wicked borrows, and will not repay;
The righteous man is gracious, and doth give.
22. Because his blest ones shall possess the earth,
Whereas his curst ones are to be cut off.
23. 'Tis from Jehovah that a good man's steps
Are settled, and he in his way delights.
24. Though he may fall, he shall not be cast out,
For still Jehovah holdeth up his hand.
25. I have been young, now also am grown old,
But have not seen a righteous man forsook,
Nor seed of him inquiring after bread.
26. He all the day is gracious, and doth lend;
Also his seed shall for a blessing be.
27. Depart from ill, and be thou doing good,
And dwell for evermore.
28. Because Jehovah loveth judgement just,
And he will not forsake his saintly ones:
For ever they've been kept;
While seed of wicked men has been cut off.
29. The righteous ones shall be possessing earth,

And they shall dwell for ever upon it.
30. A righteous mouth will utter what is wise,
So will his tongue be speaking what is just.
31. The doctrine of his God is in his heart,
There shall not any of his goings slide.
32. The wicked watcheth at the righteous man,
And will be seeking to obtain his death.
33. Jehovah will not leave him in his hand,
Nor will condemn him in his being judged.
34. Wait for Jehovah, and keep thou his way,
And he'll exalt thee to possess the earth:
Off-cutting of the wicked thou shalt see.
35. I've seen a wicked man, tyrannical,
And spreading broad like a green native tree:
36. But he will pass, and lo! he is no more;
Yea, though I seek him, nought of him is found.
37. Mark thou the perfect, see the upright man,
That unto each the latter end is peace.
38. But trespassers have been destroyed together;
The wickeds' latter end hath been cut off,
39. While righteous men have safety through Jehovah,
Their source of strength in season of distress.
40. Jehovah will help them, and set them free,
Free them from wicked men, and keep them safe
As shelterers in him.

PSALM XXXVIII.

1. JEHOVAH! not in anger check thou me;
Nor in thy hot wrath do thou chasten me.
2. For down thine arrows are come into me,
And down upon me there will come thy hand.
3. There is not any soundness in my flesh
Because of thine indignancy;

There is not any welfare in my bones
  Because of mine own sinfulness.
4. For mine iniquities go o'er my head;
  Like weighty load they weigh too much for me.
5. My scars are stinking suppurating wounds
  Because of mine own foolishness.
6. I am distorted; I bow very low;
  Through all the day in mourning I have gone,
7. Because my loins are full of loathsomeness,
  And there is nought of soundness in my flesh.
8. I am benumbed, and bruised exceedingly;
  I roar from the disquiet of my heart.
9. Great Lord! before thee is my whole desire;
  My sighing too from thee hath not been hid.
10. My heart beats fitfully; gone is my strength;
  And brightness of mine eyes; yea, even these
    Are not with me.
11.   My lovers and my friends
  Aloof from mine afflictive stroke will stand;
  Also my neighbours afar off have stood.
12. And snares are laid by them who seek my soul;
  And they who fain would hurt me speak of crimes;
  And of deceits through all the day they muse.
13. But I, as one who's deaf, I will not hear;
  And as a dumb one will not ope his mouth,
14. So I'll be like a man who heareth not,
  And in the mouth of whom are no reproofs.
15. For toward thee, Jehovah, I have hoped;
  Thou, thou wilt answer, O great Lord, my God.
16. For I have said, Lest they be glad at me:
  When my foot moved, they o'er me greatly swelled;
17. Because that I to limping was confirmed,
  And pain would be before me constantly.
18. But mine iniquity I will show out;

      I will with care avoid my sinfulness.
19. Whereas my deadly enemies are strong,
      And many are those falsely hating me.
20. And they, repaying ill instead of good,
      Oppose me while I am pursuing good.
21. Do thou be not forsaking me, Jehovah;
      My God, do thou be not afar from me.
22.   Be hasting to my help,
           Great Lord, my Saviour.

PSALM XXXIX.

1. I SAID, I will keep watch upon my ways,
    So that I be not sinning with my tongue;
    I will be keeping on my mouth a curb
    While there's a wicked man in front of me.
2. I became dumb in utter silentness;
        I held my peace from good,
        And so my pain was stirred.
3. Hot did my heart grow in the midst of me;
    Through my deep-musing plaint would burn a fire;
        Then spake I with my tongue.
4. Do thou, Jehovah, make me know mine end,
    And measure of my days, what that may be.
    I would be knowing how short-lived I am.
5. Behold! as handbreadths thou hast dealt my days;
    My lifetime is as nothing before thee;
    Surely all vanity all mankind stands.   Selah.
6. Surely in phantom each man walks about;
    Surely for vanity they make a stir;
    He hoards, but knows not who will gather them.
7. And now, what have I waited for, great Lord?
        My hope to thee is set;
8. From all my trespasses O rescue me;

As a reproach of fools expose me not.
9. I am made dumb; I will not ope my mouth,
For thou, thou wast the doer.
10. Remove from off me thine afflictive stroke;
From action of thy hand
I, I have wasting been.
11. Thou with reproofs upon iniquity
Hast been chastising man;
And thou wilt melt like moth his fond desire;
Surely all men are vanity.
12. Do thou, Jehovah, listen to my prayer;
And to my cry for help do thou give ear;
Unto my tears do thou not heedless be;
Because a sojourner am I with thee,
A pilgrim as were all my forefathers.
13. O spare me, that I may be cheering up
Before I must go hence, and be no more.

PSALM XL.

1. Waiting, I have been waiting for Jehovah,
And he'll incline to me, and hear my cry;
2. And will upbring me out of noisome pit,
Out of the miry clay;
And will make stand upon a crag my feet,
Setting my goings firm:
3. And he will put a new song in my mouth,
Praises unto our God;
Many shall see, and fearing reverently
Will in Jehovah trust.
4. O happy is that man
Who sets Jehovah for his trusted One,
And hath not turned toward presumptuous men
Or false apostasies.

5. Full many things hast thou performed, yea, thou,
   Jehovah, mine own God;
 Thy wonders and thy projects toward us
   None can detail to thee:
 I would be showing and be speaking forth;
   They're more than can be told.
6. No sacrifice or gift gave thee delight;
   Ears thou didst bore for me;
 No burnt or sin offering didst thou require.
7. Then did I say, Behold me! I am come,
 Within the book-roll it is writ of me,
8.   To do the will of thee,
   My God, I take delight:
 Also thy doctrine is in midst of me.
9. I have preached rightly in assembly great;
 Behold! my lips I will not keep restrained;
 As thou, Jehovah, thou hast fully known.
10. Thy righteousness I have not covered up
   In midst of mine own heart;
 Thy faithfulness and saving grace I've told;
 I've not concealed thy mercy and thy truth
   To the assembly great.
11.   Thou, O Jehovah, thou
 Wilt not restrain thy tender love from me;
   Thy mercy and thy truth
   Always will me preserve.
12. Yet gathering over me there have been ills
   Till they be numberless;
 Mine own iniquities o'ertaking me
   So that I cannot see;
 They muster more than hairs upon my head,
   And my heart faileth me.
13. Be thou, Jehovah, pleased to rescue me;
 Jehovah, to my help do thou make haste.

14. Those shall be shamed together and dismayed
    Who seek my soul to bring it to an end:
    Those shall be turned backward and disgraced
        Who in my hurt delight.
15. Those shall be desolate as well as shamed
    Whose saying to me is, Aha, aha!
16. Joyful shall be and gladdening in thee
        All who are seeking thee:
        Those constantly will say,
        Great will Jehovah be,
    Who are the lovers of thy saving grace.
17. And as for me, afflicted and in need,
        The Sovran Lord will think on me;
    My helper and deliverer art thou;
        My God, do thou make no delay.

PSALM XLI.

1. HAPPY is he who wisely treats the poor:
   In day of harm Jehovah will free him.
2. Jehovah will keep him, and quicken him:
        Happy on earth he'll be;
   And thou'lt not yield him to his enemies' lust.
3. Jehovah will prop him on languor's couch:
   Thou all his bed didst turn when he was sick.
4. I, I have said, Jehovah, show me grace;
   O heal my soul, for I have sinned to thee.
5. Mine enemies say wickedly of me,
   When will he die, and perished be his name?
6. And if one come to see, with empty talk
   His heart will be agathering mischief in;
   He will go out, and gossip in the street.
7. In groups against me will be whispering
        My haters all;

Against me they will purpose harm to me.
8. A thing of Belial is poured into him;
And being laid, he shall rise up no more.
9. Yea, my familiar friend,
He whom I trusted in,
One eating of my bread,
He hath uplifted against me his heel.
10. But thou, do thou, Jehovah,
Be showing grace to me, and make me rise,
And I shall be requiting them.
11. By this I've known of thy delight in me,
That none shall shout as enemy o'er me.
12. But me in my completeness thou hast held,
To make me stand before thee evermore.
13. Blest be Jehovah, God of Israel,
Through all time past and through all time to come,
Amen, yea, and amen.

PSALM XLII.

1. Like as the hart will pant along the water-brooks,
So will my soul be panting toward thee, great God.
2. Thirsting hath been my soul for God, the living God:
O when shall I go in, appearing before God?
3. My tears have been to me as bread both day and night,
While it was said to me all day, Where is thy God?
4. These things I'll call to mind, and will pour out my soul
When passing with the crowd,
I march them up unto the house of God,
With voice of song and thanks, a festal multitude.
5. Why wilt thou be down-bowing, O my soul,
Disquieted in me?
Hope thou in the great God, for yet I will thank him
His face's saving help.

6. My God, within me will my soul down-bow itself:
   Therefore I will remember thee from Jordan land,
       And from the Hermonites; from Mizar hill.
7. Deep unto deep resounds thy voice of waterspouts;
   Thy breakers all and billows over me are gone.
8. By day Jehovah will command his mercy forth,
       And in the night shall singing be with me,
           Prayer to my God of life.
9. I'll cry to God my crag, O why forget'st thou me?
   Why mourning must I go, oppressed by enemy?
10. With murder in my bones my troublers taunted me,
    While saying to me all the day, Where is thy God?
11.   Why wilt thou be down-bowing, O my soul,
            And why disquieted in me?
        Hope thou in the great God, for yet I will thank him,
        My face's saving helper and my God.

PSALM XLIII.

1. Judge me, O thou great God, and vindicate my cause
       From an ungracious folk;
   From man deceitful and unjust, O keep me free.
2.   For it is thou who art my God of strength;
          Why hast thou spurned me off?
      Wherefore in mourning must I walk about
          Oppressed by enemy?
3.   O do thou send thy light forth and thy truth;
          They, they shall lead me on:
      They shall inbring me to thy holy hill
          And to thy dwelling-place.
4.   And I shall go to altar of great God,
          To God, my chiefest joy;
      And will thank thee with harp,
          O thou great God, my God.

5. Why wilt thou be down-bowing, O my soul,
    And why disquieted in me?
  Hope thou in the great God, for yet I will thank him,
    My face's saving helper and my God.

PSALM XLIV.

1. Great God, we with our ears have listened to,
   Our forefathers have often told to us,
   The working which thou wroughtest in their day,
    In days of olden time.
2.   'Twas thou who with thy hand
   Didst pluck out nations, and wouldst plant in them;
   Wouldst blight down peoples, and wouldst send in them.
3. For not by their own sword gat they the land,
   Nor was their arm a saving help to them;
   But the right hand of thee, and arm of thee,
   And light of thy face, when thou favouredst them.
4. Thou, even thou art he, my King, great God;
   Command salvations unto Jacob's folk.
5. Through thee our harassers we'll backward push;
   Through thy name we shall tread insurgents down.
6. For not in mine own bow will I confide,
   Nor can a sword of mine be saving me,
7. But thou hast saved us from our harassers,
   And them who hate us thou hast put to shame.
8. In God we have been praising all the day;
   And to thy name we ever will give thanks.   Selah.
9. Yet thou hast spurned, and art disgracing us;
   And thou wilt not go forward with our hosts:
10. Thou wilt make us retreat before the foe;
   And those who hate have spoiled us for themselves.
11. Thou wilt give us like sheep to be devoured,
   And 'mid the heathen thou hast scattered us.

12. Thou wilt sell off thy people without stint,
    And hast made no increasing of their price.
13. Thou'lt set us a reproach of dwellers here,
    A scorn and mock of dwellers round about.
14. Thou'lt set us for a byword among nations,
    A wagging of the head among the peoples.
15. All day is my disgrace in front of me;
    And shaming of my face hath covered me;
16. From voices of reproach and blasphemy;
    From face of enemy and vengeful man.
17.   All this hath come on us,
        And we forgat not thee;
    Nor have done falsely with thy covenant:
18. Not backward has our heart been turned away,
    Nor hath our going slanted from thy path,
19. That thou hast bruised us in a place of dragons,
    And wilt o'erpall us with the shade of death.
20. If we forgat the name of our own God,
    And would spread out our hands to a strange god,
21. Would not great God be searching into this?
    For he well knows the secrets of the heart.
22. Yea, for thy cause we have been killed all day,
    We have been deemed as sheep for slaughtering.
23. Arouse thee! wherefore wilt thou sleep, great Lord!
    Awake! do not be spurning utterly!
24. O wherefore wilt thou keep thy face concealed?
    Wilt thou forget us humbled and oppressed?
25. For bowing down to dust hath been our soul,
    Close-clinging earthward has our belly been.
26. Arise! do thou be helpful unto us!
    And do redeem us for thy mercy's sake.

PSALM XLV.

1. My heart hath been preparing a choice theme;
   Now do I say my tribute to a king;
   My tongue the pen of one who swift can write.
2. Thou'rt fairer far than children of mankind;
   Grace hath been poured into the lips of thee;
   Therefore great God hath blessed thee for aye.
3. Engird thy sword on thigh, O mighty One!
   Amid thine honour and thy majesty:
4. And in thy majesty ride prosperously
   Because of truth and humble righteousness:
   And thy right hand shall teach thee fearful things.
5.   Thine arrows being sharp,
   The peoples underneath thee shall fall down,
   Who are in heart the enemies of the King.
6. Thy throne, great God, for ever doth endure;
   A sceptre straight is sceptre of thy realm.
7. Thou lovest right, and hatest wickedness;
   Therefore hath God, thy God anointed thee
   With oil of joy above thy fellow-men.
8. Of myrrh and aloes, and of cassia spice
         Do all thy garments smell;
   From ivory halls hath music gladdened thee.
9. Daughters of kings are with thy valued ones;
   The queen is standing up at thy right hand
         In Ophir's purest gold.
10. Hearken, O daughter, see, and lend thine ear;
    Forget thy people and thy father's house;
11. And let the King desire thy beauteousness;
          For he is thy great Lord,
          And do thou worship him.
12. And Tyrus' daughter coming with a gift,
    The rich ones of the folk will court thy smile.

13. All glorious the King's daughter is within;
    Of gold embroidery is her attire:
14. Arrayed she shall be led up to the King;
    The virgins after her, as friends of her,
        Being brought in to thee.
15. They shall be led with gladsomeness and joy;
    Shall be brought in to palace of the King.
16. Where stood thy fathers, there shall be thy sons,
    Whom thou wilt set for chiefs in all the earth.
17. I'll keep in mind thy name from age to age;
    Therefore shall peoples render thanks to thee
        For ever evermore.

PSALM XLVI.

1. GREAT God, for us a shelter, and a strength,
   A help in troubles hath been found full oft.
2. Therefore we will not fear, though earth be changed,
   Though hills be moved into the heart of seas:
3. Though restless, turbid may its waters be;
   Though quaking be the hills in its proud swell.   Selah.
4.   A river is
   Whose rills will glad the city of great God,
   The holy dwelling-place of him Most High.
5. Great God within her, she shall not be moved;
   Help her great God will, at the dawn of morn.
6. Restless were nations, kingdoms were astir;
   He hath sent forth his voice, the earth will melt.
7. Jehovah of the hosts is on our side;
   A safe high-place for us is Jacob's God.   Selah.
8. O come ye, gaze at doings of Jehovah,
   What desolations he hath made on earth!
9.   A silencer of wars
           Unto the ends of earth.

The bow he'll shatter, and he'll cut the spear:
The rolling chariot he will burn in fire.
10. Slack ye, and know that I who am great God,
I shall be high 'mong nations, high on earth.
11. Jehovah of the hosts is on our side;
A safe high-place for us is Jacob's God.   Selah.

PSALM XLVII.

1. O ALL ye peoples, be ye clapping hands!
Shout to great God with voice of lively song!
2. Because Jehovah the Most High, the Feared,
Is King of greatness over all the earth.
3. He will subject the peoples under us,
Also the nations underneath our feet.
4. He will choose out for us our heritage,
The goodly lot of Jacob whom he loved.   Selah.
5. Upward great God hath gone amid a shout;
Jehovah 'mid the voice of trumpeting.
6. Attune your psalms of God; attune your psalms;
Tune psalms unto our King; attune your psalms.
7. For King of all the earth is the great God;
Tune your instructive psalm.
8. His reign o'er nations the great God hath held;
Great God hath sat upon his holy throne.
9. Nobles of peoples have been gathered in,
As people of the God of Abraham;
For to great God belong the shields of earth;
Highly is he gone up.

PSALM XLVIII.

1. GREAT is Jehovah, and supremely praised
In city of our God, his holy mount.

2. Ah! beauteous prospect, joy of all the earth,
   The mount of Zion, the side-parts of north,
       The town of the great King.
3. Great God within the palaces of her
       A known high refuge is.
4. For lo! what time the kings confederate met,
       They passed together by;
5. They, when they saw, at once they were amazed,
   Were sorely troubled, were gone off in haste.
6. A trembling fit took hold upon them there
       Like travailing woman's pangs.
7.   Thou with a wind from east
   Wouldst break the ships of Tarshish thoroughly.
8. As we have heard, so also we have seen
   In city of Jehovah of the hosts,
       In city of our God;
   Great God will stablish her for evermore.   Selah.
9. We have adored thy mercy, O great God,
       In midst of thine own temple.
10.   Like as thy name, great God,
   So is thy praise upon the ends of earth;
   Of righteousness thine own right hand is full.
11.   Glad shall mount Zion be;
   Rejoicing shall the Judah daughters be
       For judgements thou hast wrought.
12. Walk around Zion and encircle her;
       Count ye the towers thereof;
13. Apply your heart unto her battlement;
       Survey her palaces;
   That so ye may tell forth to future race
14.   How this, who is great God,
   Is also our own God for evermore.
   'Tis he who will conduct us over death.

PSALM XLIX.

1. O LISTEN unto this, ye peoples all!
   Give ear, all ye the sojourners of time!
2. Whether the sons of low, or sons of high;
   At once the rich man, and the needy one.
3. My mouth shall be discoursing matters wise;
   And musings of my heart are pondered well.
4. I'll lend unto a parable mine ear;
   I'll open on the harp my riddle dark.
5. Why should I fear that in the days of ill
   Iniquity may come around my heels?
6. They who confide in substance of their own,
   And in abounding riches boast themselves,
7. A brother no man can at all redeem,
   Or give to God atonement for himself.
8. And costly is redemption of their soul;
   When that had ceased for aye,
9. Then might he still live on continuously,
   He might not see corruption.
10. But he shall see that wise men are to die;
    That fool and brutish both are perishing,
    And leave their substance to succeeding ones.
11. They inly think their houses are for aye,
    Their dwellings are to be from age to age;
    They've called their own names upon bits of land.
12. But man in eminence would not abide;
    He's classified like beasts to silence gone.
13. Such is their way; a folly for themselves;
    Yet their successors with their mouths approve. Selah.
14. Like flock of sheep to Sheol they've set out;
    'Tis death will shepherd them;
    And upright ones shall rule o'er them at morn,
    Their frame too must in Sheol wear away,

A lingering home for it.
15.   Ah! but great God
He will redeem my soul from Sheol's hand,
    When he will take me hence.   Selah.
16. Do not thou fear when one shall be enriched,
    When is increased the glory of his house;
17. For through his death he can take nothing hence,
    Nor down shall move his glory after him.
18. Although his soul in lifetime he would bless,
    And men will praise thee doing well for self,
19. It shall go in among his father's race;
    Perpetually they shall not see the light.
20. Man eminent, who will not understand,
    Is classified like beasts to silence gone.

PSALM L.

1. God, the great God, Jehovah hath spoke out,
        And he will call the earth,
    From rising of the sun to where it sets.
2. From out of Zion, beauty's perfectness,
        Great God hath shinèd forth.
3. Our God will come, and will not heedless be;
    A fire before his presence shall devour,
    And round about him a wild storm hath raged.
4. He will be calling to the heavens above,
    And to the earth, that he may right his folk.
5. Gather ye unto me my saintly ones
    Who keep my covenant through sacrifice.
6. Then heavens will display his righteousness;
    Because that the great God himself is Judge.   Selah.
7. Hear, O my people, and I will speak out;
    O Israël, I'll witness against thee:
    Great God, thine own God, verily am I.

8. Not for thy sacrifices check I thee,
   Or thy burnt-gifts before me constantly:
9. I will not take from house of thine a bull,
   Nor yet he-goats from folding-pens of thine.
10. For mine is every forest animal,
    The cattle upon mountains thousandfold;
11. Well do I know each flier of the hills;
    And roamers of the field are at my call.
12. If I were hungry, I would not tell thee;
    For mine the world and fulness thereof are.
13. Shall I be eating of the flesh of bulls?
    Or of the blood of he-goats shall I drink?
14. Offer to God the sacrifice of thanks,
    Also perform to the Most High thy vows.
15. And call thou upon me in troublous day;
    I'll pull thee out, and thou shalt honour me.
16. But to the wicked man great God hath said,
    What right hast thou to rhyme my statutes o'er,
    Or to take up my covenant in thy mouth?
17. Yea, thou who hast been hating chastisement,
    And who wilt throw my words behind thy back.
18. Seeing a thief, thou wouldst consent with him,
    And with adulterers hast had thy part.
19. Thy mouth thou hast been sending into ill;
    Also thy tongue will fabricate deceit:
20. Thou sitting, wilt against thy brother speak;
    Against thy mother's son thou slanderest.
21. These thou hast done, and I have kept aloof;
    Thou thought'st I should be merely like thyself:
    I'll check thee, and array before thine eyes.
22. Consider this now, ye forgetting God,
    Lest I should tear when there's no rescuer.
23. An offerer of thanks will honour me;
    And when he hath set way,
    I'll make him see the saving grace of God.

PSALM LI.

1. Show grace to me, great God, for mercy's sake;
   In thy much love blot out my trespasses.
2. Me throughly wash from mine iniquity;
   And from my sinfulness O cleanse thou me.
3. For I my trespasses will fully know,
   My sin too is before me constantly.
4. It is to thee, thee only, I have sinned,
   And evilly in thy sight I have done;
   That so thou shalt be righteous when thou speakest,
   And clear when thou wilt judge.
5. Lo! in iniquity I was brought forth;
   Also in sin my mother me conceived.
6. Lo! truth thou hast desired in inward parts;
   Wisdom in privacy thou'lt make me know.
7. Thou wilt purge me with hyssop till I'm clean;
   Thou'lt wash me till I'm whiter than the snow;
8. Thou'lt make me hear of joy and gladsomeness;
   So shall rejoice the bones which thou didst bruise.
9. O do thou hide thy presence from my sins!
   All mine iniquities do thou blot out!
10. A clean heart do create for me, O God!
    A steadfast spirit within me renew!
11. Do thou not cast me from before thy face:
    Thy Holy Spirit do not take from me.
12. Restore to me thy joyful saving grace;
    And let a willing spirit hold me up.
13. I will be teaching trespassers thy ways,
    And sinners unto thee shall turn again.
14. Absolve me from bloodguiltiness, great God,
    My God of saving grace;
    My tongue shall brightly sing thy righteousness.
15. O Sovran Lord, these lips of mine thou'lt ope,

And then my mouth shall manifest thy praise.
16. For thou wilt not delight in sacrifice,
  Although I fain would give;
In offerings-burnt no pleasure thou wilt have.
17. God's sacrifices are a broken spirit;
  A broken contrite heart
  Thou, God, wilt not despise.
18. Do good to Zion which thou favourest;
Build up the ramparts of Jerusalem.
19. Then thou'lt delight in righteous sacrifice,
  In offerings burnt and whole;
Then shall go up upon thine altar, bulls.

PSALM LII.

1. WHY wilt thou boast in evil, lordly man?
The Almighty's mercy lasteth all the day.
2. Malicious deeds thou wilt devise, thy tongue
Like razor whetted, working guilefully.
3. Thou hast been loving evil more than good;
Falsity more than speaking righteousness.   Selah.
4. Thou hast been loving all-devouring words,
  O thou deceitful tongue.
5. Surely will God down-break thee utterly,
Remove thee quick, and tear thee out of tent,
And root thee up out of the land of life.   Selah.
6. Then shall the righteous see, and they shall fear,
  And over him they'll laugh.
7.   Behold the lordly man!
Who would not take great God to be his strength,
But would confide in his abounding wealth:
  Would strengthen through his malice.
8. While I, yea, I, like a green olive-tree
  Am in the house of God;

I have put trust in mercy of great God,
    As lasting evermore.
9. I'll thank thee ever for what thou hast done;
  And will await thy name, for it is good,
    In presence of thy saints.

PSALM LIII.

1. THE fool saith in his heart, There is no God;
  They work corrupt abominable wrong;
    There's no one doing good.
2. Great God from out of heaven hath looked down
    Upon the sons of men,
  To see if there was any well inclined,
    Inquiring after God.
3. The whole's gone off; they're putrid through and through;
    There's no one doing good,
    There is not even one.
4. Was there no knowledge in these wrongdoers?
  Eating my people, they have eaten bread;
    God they have not invoked.
5. There they did dread a dread; no dread had been.
  But God had scattered thy encamper's bones:
  Thou didst beshame, for God rejected them.
6.   Who will from Zion give
    Safe help to Israël?
  When the great God brings back his captive folk,
  Jacob shall joy, and Israel be glad.

PSALM LIV.

1. GREAT God, by thine own name be saving me;
  And by thy might be thou redressing me.
2. Great God, do thou be listening my prayer;

    Be giving ear to sayings of my mouth.
3. For aliens have been rising up at me,
    And tyrants have been seeking for my soul;
    They have not set great God in front of them.   Selah.
4. Behold! great God is giving help to me;
    Great Lord is with upholders of my soul.
5. He'll back this evil on my spying foes;
    In thine own truth be thou suppressing them.
6. With freeness I will sacrifice to thee;
    Will thank thy name, Jehovah, for 'tis good.
7. For he from all distress hath rescued me:
    And through mine enemies mine eye hath seen.

PSALM LV.

1. Do thou give ear, great God, unto my prayer;
    And hide thee not from my beseeching cry:
2. Do thou attend to me, and answer me;
    I'm restless in my plaint, and toss about,
3.   From voice of enemy,
    From presence of oppressive wicked man;
    For they will move against me godlessness,
    And will in anger be opposing me.
4. My heart is giving pain in midst of me,
    And terrorings of death are fallen on me;
5. Fearing and trembling will come into me;
    And there will cover me a shuddering dread.
6.   So that I say,
    Who will give me a pinion like the dove?
    I fain would fly, and find a dwelling-place.
7. Behold! I would be flitting off afar,
        Would lodge in wilderness.   Selah.
8. I would be making haste for my escape
    Out of the rushing wind, out of the storm.

9. Upswallow thou, O Lord! divide their tongue;
 For in the city I've seen crime and strife.
10.   By day as well as night
 They will go round upon the walls thereof;
 And vice and misery are in her midst.
11.   Great wrongs are in her midst;
 And there is no removing from her streets
          Fraud and deceitfulness.
12. Yet 'twas no enemy reproaching me,
          I would bear that:
 It was no hater swelling up at me,
          I would have hid from him.
13. But it was thou, a man in mine esteem,
 One of my trained men and acquaintances,
14. With whom together we held counsel sweet;
 In house of God we walked amid the throng.
15.   Death shall be seizing them!
 Down into Sheol they shall go alive,
 For evils in their dwelling, in their midst.
16. But I, unto the great Lord I will call,
 So that Jehovah may be saving me.
17. At evening, and at morning, and at noon,
 I will be plaintive, and disquieted;
          And he will hear my voice.
18. He hath redeemed to peacefulness my soul
          From conflict which I had,
 Because full many have been they with me.
19. The Almighty One will hear and answer them;
          He sitting from of old,   Selah.
 Even them by whom no changes have been felt,
 And who have not been fearing the great God.
20. He put his hands forth at his wellwishers;
          He brake his covenant;
21. Though smooth have been the butterings of his mouth,

'Tis conflict in his heart:
Although his words have softer been than oil,
Yet these are swords unsheathed.
22. Cast on Jehovah what is laid to thee,
And he will bear thee through:
He'll never let the righteous man be moved.
23. But thou, great God, thou wilt make them go down
Into corruption's pit;
The men of bloodiness and of deceit
Shall not live half their days.
But I shall put my trust in thee.

PSALM LVI.

1. Show grace to me, great God,
For man hath hunted me:
He all the day with fight oppresseth me.
2. My spying foes have hunted me all day;
For many fight against me, O Most High.
3. What day I fear
I will to thee direct my confidence.
4. In God I shall be praising his own word;
In God I do confide; I shall not fear;
What thing is there that flesh can do to me?
5. Through all the day my words they will distort;
Against me all their thinkings are for ill.
6. Clubbing together, hiding themselves close,
Will they, yea, they upon my heels keep watch,
As if they have been waiting for my soul.
7. For wrongfulness do thou deal forth at them!
In anger bring the peoples down, O God!
8. My wanderings thou hast reckoned up, yea, thou:
O do thou put my tears into thy bottle;
Are they not in thy book?

9. Then shall mine enemies be turned aback
     In day when I shall call;
   This I have known, for God is toward me.
10. Through the great God I'll give the matter praise,
    I through Jehovah will the matter praise.
11. In God I do confide; I shall not fear;
    What is there that mankind can do to me?
12. On me, O thou great God, have been thy vows;
    I shall be paying thanksgivings to thee.
13. Since thou delivered hast my soul from death,
    Wilt thou not keep my feet from overthrow?
    To walk about in presence of great God
       In light of living men.

PSALM LVII.

1. Show grace to me, great God; show grace to me;
   Because in thee is sheltering my soul:
   And in thy wings' shade I will shelter keep
   Until these outrages be overpast.
2. I will be calling unto God Most High,
   To the Almighty who completes for me.
3. He'll send from heaven, and be saving me;
        My chaser hath reproached;   Selah.
   Great God will send his mercy and his truth.
4. My soul in midst of lions I could lay;
       Those blazing sons of men,
   The teeth of whom a spear and arrows be,
   Also their tongue is a keen-cutting sword.
5. Be thou exalted above heavens, great God;
   Above the whole of earth thy gloriousness.
6. A net did they make ready for my steps;
       He did bow down my soul;
   They dug before the face of me a ditch;

They fell right into it.   Selah.
7. Established hath my heart been, O great God;
    Established is my heart:
  I will be singing and attuning psalms.
8.   Awake thou, O my tongue!
  Do thou awake the psaltery and harp!
    I will awake the dawn.
9. I'll thank thee among nations, Sovran Lord:
  I will tune psalms of thee among the folks.
10. For great unto the heavens thy mercy is,
  Also unto the skies hath been thy truth.
11. Be thou exalted above heavens, great God,
  Above the whole of earth thy gloriousness.

PSALM LVIII.

1. Is it indeed, O rulers, righteously ye speak?
  Is it uprightly ye will judge, O sons of men?
2. Nay, even with the heart perversely ye will act;
  Ye will cause earth to feel your violence of hands.
3. Estranged have been the wicked from the very womb;
  Awandering they have gone from birthtime, speaking lies.
4. A furiousness have they like fury of the snake;
  Like as an adder deaf he will close up his ear,
5. So that he shall not hear the voice of whisperers,
  Of one who charmeth charms with wisdom's skilfulness.
6. Great God, do thou break down the teeth within their mouth;
  The fang-teeth of young lions shatter thou, Jehovah!
7. They shall be loathed like waters, they shall go their way;
  He'll guide his arrows so as if they'd mow themselves.
8. Like as a trail of melting slime he shall go off;
  Like childbirth immature, they've not beheld the sun.
9. Before your cooking-pots shall feel the bramble warm,
  Though live, or though red-hot, he'll blow it clean away.

10. Glad will the righteous be when vengeance he beholds;
His footsteps he shall wash with blood of wicked men.
11. And men will say, Ah! fruit is for the righteous man.
Ah! verily great God is judging in the earth.

PSALM LIX.

1. Outrid me from mine enemies, my God!
From mine insurgents set thou me on high!
2. Outrid me from ungodly wrongdoers!
And from bloodthirsty men, O save thou me!
3. For lo! they've lain in ambush for my soul:
Against me strong ones will together club;
Not for my trespass, or my sin, Jehovah.
4. For no ill done, they'll run and be prepared;
O rouse thou up to meet me, and to see!
5. And thou, Jehovah, the great God of hosts,
The God of Israël,
Do thou awake to visit nations all:
No grace give thou to any traitors vile.   Selah.
6. They will return at eve, will prowl like dogs,
And round the city go.
7. Behold! they will fast utter with their mouth;
While swords are also in the lips of them;
For who is there that hears?
8. But thou, Jehovah, thou wilt laugh at them:
Thou wilt be mocking at the nations all.
9. His strength I unto thee will keep in watch;
For the great God shall be my height secure.
10. My God of mercy will before me come;
God will make me see through my spying foes.
11. Do not thou slay them, lest my folk forget:
Shake thou them with thy force, and bring them down.
O thou our shield, great Lord!

12. What sin of mouth! what language of their lips!
    And when they shall be taken in their pride,
    What cursing and what falsehood they will use!
13. Consume in wrath! consume till they be not!
    And men shall know that the great God doth rule
    Through Jacob to the endings of the earth.   Selah.
14. So they may come each eve, may prowl like dogs,
    And round the city go.
15. They, they shall roam unquietly for food;
    And though unsatisfied, shall so remain.
16. But I, I will be singing of thy strength,
    And of thy mercy I will chant at morn;
    Since thou hast been a height secure for me,
    And place of refuge in my troublous day.
17. My strength I unto thee will tune in psalms;
    For the great God hath been my height secure,
    Hath been my God of mercy.

PSALM LX.

1. Thou, God, hast spurned us off, hast battered us!
   Thou hast been angry; O return to us.
2. Thou hast bequaked the earth, hast riven it;
   O heal the breaks thereof, for it hath moved.
3. Thou hast compelled thy folk to see hard things,
   Hast made us drink a wine of staggering!
4. Thou gavest to those fearing thee a flag
   For its displayal in behalf of truth.   Selah.
5. That thy beloved ones may be pulled through,
   O save with thy right hand, and answer me.
6. Great God hath spoken in his holiness;
   I will exult; I'll portion Shechem out;
   And Succoth's valley I will measure up.
7. Gilead is mine; Manasseh too is mine;

        And Ephraim is the stronghold of my head;
            Judah my lawgiver,
8.   Moab my washing-pan;
    Out over Edom I will cast my shoe;
    For me, Philistia, raise thy joyful shout.
9. Who will conduct me to the city fenced?
    Who hath up-led me unto Edom land?
10. But thou, great God, thou who hast spurned us off,
    And wilt not go, O God, before our hosts?
11. Vouchsafe to us a helping from distress;
    For worthless is the saving help of man.
12. Through the great God shall we do valiantly;
    And he, yea, he will tread our troublers down.

PSALM LXI.

1. Do thou, great God, be hearing mine outcry;
   Do thou be giving heed unto my prayer.
2. From end of earth I unto thee will call
       When feeble is my heart:
   To rock high up above me, lead thou me.
3. For thou hast been a shelter unto me;
   A tower of strength from face of enemy.
4. I will sojourn within thy tent for aye;
   Will shelter in the covert of thy wings.   Selah.
5.   Because that thou,
   Yea, thou, great God, hast hearkened to my vows;
   Hast portioned like the fearers of thy name.
6. Days to the days of kingship thou wilt add;
   The royal years like race succeeding race.
7. He'll sit for aye in presence of great God;
   Mercy and truth supplied for keeping him.
8. So I will tune thy name until the end,
   While I perform my vows from day to day.

PSALM LXII.

1. Ah! toward God in silence waits my soul;
    It is from him that my salvation comes.
2. Ah! he my rock and my salvation is;
    My height secure; I shall not much be moved.
3. How long will ye conspire against a man?
        Slain shall be all of you,
    Like wall o'erbent, a fence that's driven down.
4.   Ah! from his dignity
        They've planned to drive him off:
    They favour lying; with the mouth they'll bless,
        But inwardly they'll curse.   Selah.
5. Ah! unto God look silently, my soul;
    Because from him my expectation is.
6. Ah! he my rock and my salvation is;
    My height secure; I shall not be removed.
7. On God my safety and my glory rest;
    My rock of strength, my shelter is in God.
8. Confide in him at all times, O ye folk;
    Be pouring out before his face your heart;
    Great God shall be a shelter unto us.   Selah.
9. Ah! vanity are sons of man low-born;
        Mere lie are sons high-born:
    They in the balances to go aloft,
    They shall at once be less than vanity.
10. Be not confiding in oppressiveness;
    Nor yet in robbery do ye be vain;
        On force, when it may grow,
        Be not ye setting heart.
11. One thing there is which the great Lord did speak;
    Two things there be which I have listened to:
        That strength belongs to God;

12. Also to thee, Lord, mercy doth belong:
  For thou, yea, thou
 Wilt pay to each man as his work hath been.

PSALM LXIII.

1. Great God, my God art thou;
  Thee I will early seek;
  My soul doth thirst for thee;
  My flesh doth long for thee
 In dry and weary land where waters fail,
2. As in the holy place I've gazed on thee,
 To see thy power and thy gloriousness.
3. Since better is thy mercy than is life,
 My lips shall busily be lauding thee.
4. So I will bless thee while I am in life;
 In name of thee I will lift up my hands.
5. Like as with richest marrow and with fat
  My soul shall be sufficed;
 And with bright-singing lips my mouth shall praise.
6. When I've remembered thee upon my bed,
 In the night-watches I would muse on thee.
7. Since thou hast been a helper unto me,
 In shadow of thy wings I'll brightly sing.
8. My soul hath been close-clinging after thee;
 On me hath thy right hand been keeping hold.
9. But they to ruin, they will seek my soul;
 They shall go in to lowest parts of earth.
10. They would make him run out on slaying sword;
 A portion for the jackals they shall be.
11. Whereas the king shall gladden in great God;
 Glory shall every one who swears by him;
 For stopped shall be the mouth that speaks false words.

PSALM LXIV.

1. Hear thou, O God, my voice in my complaint;
   From dread of enemy preserve my life.
2. Do thou hide me from council of ill men;
   From gatherings of godless wrongdoers;
3. Those who have sharpened like the sword their tongue,
   Who have sped forth their arrow, bitter speech,
4. To shoot in secret spots the perfect man;
   They suddenly will shoot him, and not fear.
5. They'll foster for themselves an evil cause;
   They'll often talk about concealing snares;
   They've said, Who is there that will look at them?
6.   They'll search perversities;
   We have completed a most searching search;
   And inwardly each man and heart is deep.
7. But the great God will shoot at them a shaft;
   With suddenness have been the wounds of them.
8.   While they would stumble him,
           Their tongue falls on themselves.
   Away shall flit each one who looks on them.
9.   Then all mankind shall fear,
   And shall display the doing of great God,
   And they his work have better understood.
10. Glad shall the righteous man be in Jehovah,
          In whom he sheltereth;
    And glory shall all those of upright heart.

PSALM LXV.

1. To thee is silently adoring praise,
         Great God in Zion, due;
   And unto thee shall be performed the vow.
2.   O hearkener of prayer,
   In unto thee all living flesh shall come.

3. Iniquities have been too strong for me;
   Our trespasses wilt thou, yea, thou, purge off.
4. Blest he whom thou wilt choose and wilt bring near,
         He in thy courts shall dwell;
   We'll be sufficed with goodness of thy house.
         Of thine own holy temple.
5. Thou'lt fearfully yet rightly answer us,
         Our God of saving grace;
   The confidence of all the earth and sea
         Even to utmost ends.
6. Who setteth firm the mountains by his strength,
         He being girt with might;
7. Who stilleth down the uproar of the seas,
         The uproar of their waves,
         And tumult of the peoples.
8. Then fearing shall the utmost dwellers be
         By reason of thy signs;
   The outlets of the morning and the eve
         Thou wilt make jubilant.
9. Thou visitest the earth, and waterest her;
         Thou much enrichest her:
   The rill of God is full of water-flood;
         Thou wilt prepare them corn,
         When so preparing her.
10. Her furrows drenching, beating down her rigs,
    With showerings thou wilt throughly soften her;
         Her springing thou wilt bless.
11. Thou hast with thine own goodness crowned the year;
    Also thy tracks will drop down fatfulness.
12. They'll drop on pastures of the wilderness;
    Until with joy the little hills be girt.
13. Clothed have the pastures been with flocks of sheep;
    The valleys shall be covered o'er with corn;
    They will be giving shout: yea, they will sing.

PSALM LXVI.

1. O shout ye to great God o'er all the earth!
2. Do ye attune the glory of his name;
   Do ye make glorious the praise of him.
3.   Say ye unto great God,
   How terrible have been the works of thee!
         Through thine abundant strength
   Thine enemies shall cringing come to thee.
4. All on the earth shall bowing worship thee;
         And shall attune to thee;
         They shall attune thy name.   Selah.
5. Come ye and see the doings of great God,
   Fearful in action on the sons of men.
6. He turned the sea till it became dry land;
   Right through the river they shall cross on foot:
         There we were glad in him,
7. Who ruleth in his mightiness for aye;
   His eyes upon the nations will keep watch.
   Let the rebellious not exalt themselves.   Selah.
8. Give blessing, O ye nations, to our God,
   And cause be heard aloud the praise of him,
9. Who is the setter of our soul in life,
   And hath not given our foot to be removed.
10. Because thou hast been trying us, great God;
    Hast fined us like as silver is refined;
11. Hast made us go into the hunter's net;
    Hast put severe oppression on our loins:
12. Hast made a feeble man ride at our head:
    We did go through the fire and through the flood;
    But thou wouldst bring us forth to affluence.
13. I'll go into thy house with offerings-burnt;
    I will be paying unto thee my vows,
14. Even those which had been uttered by my lips,

And spoken by my mouth when in distress.
15. Offerings of fatlings I will burn to thee
    With incense fat of rams;
    I'll sacrifice both bullocks and he-goats.   Selah.
16. O come ye, hearken, and I will recount,
    All ye who fear great God,
    What things he hath been doing for my soul.
17. I unto him did call out with my mouth,
    And lofty praise was underneath my tongue.
18. Unrightness if I've seen complacently,
    The Sovran Lord will not be hearkening.
19. But truly the great God hath hearkened;
    He hath attended to my praying voice.
20.   O blessèd be great God,
    Because he hath not turned aside my prayer,
    Nor yet his grace from me.

PSALM LXVII.

1.   GREAT God,
   He will show grace to us and will bless us;
   He'll cause the shining of his face with us.   Selah.
2. So to make known throughout the earth thy way,
   Throughout all nations thine own saving grace.
3. Thanks will the peoples give to thee, great God;
   Thanks will the peoples give thee, all of them.
4. Gladsome and jubilant the folks will be;
   For thou wilt judge the peoples uprightly:
   And folks upon the earth, thou wilt them lead.   Selah.
5. Thanks shall the people give to thee, great God;
   Thanks shall the peoples give thee, all of them.
6. The earth has been bestowing her increase;
   Great God, our own God, will be blessing us;
7.   God will be blessing us,
   And all the ends of earth be fearing him.

PSALM LXVIII.

1. God will arise, his enemies will scatter;
   His haters too shall from his presence flee.
2. Like driving out of smoke, so thou wilt drive;
   Like melting down of wax before the fire,
   So shall the wicked perish before God.
3. Whereas the righteous ones shall gladsome be;
   They shall exult in presence of great God,
   And will be joyful in their gladsomeness.
4. Sing ye unto great God; attune his name!
   Cast roads for him who rides through Arabah
   By Jah his name, and triumph before him.
5. Fathering orphans, and redressing widows
   Is God in his abode of holiness:
6. Great God who makes the lonely sit in homes,
   Who brings forth prisoners to plenteous good;
   Ah! the rebellious dwell in barren drought.
7. Great God, when thou went'st forth before thy folk,
   When thou wast marching through the desert waste,   Selah.
8. The earth was quaking, yea, the heavens gave drop
       At presence of great God;
   Yon Sinai at the presence of great God,
       The God of Israël.
9. Free rain of gifts thou wilt shake out, O God;
   Thy heritage, and it was weary, thou,
       Yea, thou confirmedst it.
10. Thy company have settled down in it;
        Thou wouldst prepare, O God,
        Thy goodness for the poor.
11. The Sovran Lord himself would give the word:
    The tidings-bearers be a numerous host.
12. The kings of hosts will flit, will flit away;
    And a home-keeper, she'll divide the spoil.
13. Ye shall not lie between two boundaries;

Wings of a dove that gleams with silver gloss,
And her strong pinions with green-glinting gold.

14. When the Almighty spreadeth kings by her,
    She will cause snow in Zalmon.
15. A mountain of great God is Bashan mount;
    A mountain of high peaks is Bashan mount.
16. Why will ye grudge, ye mountains of high peaks,
    Against the mount where God desires to sit,
    Yea, where Jehovah would dwell specially?
17. The chariots of God are myriads twain,
    Thousands repeatedly;
    The Sovran Lord with them,
    Sinai in holy place.
18. Thou hast ascended to the lofty height;
    Thou hast led captive a captivity;
    Thou hast been taking gifts among mankind,
    Yea, even the rebellious ones do dwell,
    O Jah, great God.
19.   Blest be the Sovran Lord
    Who day by day is putting load on us,
    The mighty God of our deliverance.   Selah.
20.   Almighty God
    To us hath been a God of saving helps;
    Yet to Jehovah Sovran Lord belong
    The issues unto death.
21.   Ah! the great God
    Will strike the head through of his enemies.
    The hairy scalp
    That goeth on persisting in its guilt.
22. The Lord hath said, From Bashan I'll bring back,
    I will bring back from shady depths of sea;
23. That so thou mayest dash thy foot in blood,
    That tongue of dogs of thine
    From enemies may share.

24. They have beheld thy goings, O great God,
    Goings of God my King in holy place.
25. Before went singers, then stringed instruments,
    Amid a throng of damsels timbrelling.
26. In congregations bless ye the great God,
    The Sovran Lord, O ye of Israel's fount.
27. There's Benjamin, though small, their ruling one;
    The chiefs of Judah, their executor;
    Chiefs of Zebulon, chiefs of Naphtali.
28. Thy God it was who did command thy strength;
    Be strengthening, O God,
    What thou hast done for us.
29. Drawn by thy temple at Jerusalem,
    To thee shall kings be bringing up a gift.
30. Do thou rebuke the wild beasts of the reeds;
    The concourse of strong bulls with calves of people;
    Him who submits himself with silver coins;
    Scatter the peoples who delight in conflicts.
31. There shall come magnates out from Mizraim;
    Cush will run forth his hands to the great God.
32.   Ye kingdoms of the earth,
        Be singing to great God,
        Attune the Sovran Lord;   Selah.
33. To him who rides on heavens of heavens of old!
    Lo! he'll give out his voice, a voice of strength.
34.   Ascribe ye strength to the great God,
    O'er Israël is his excellency,
        His strength too in the skies.
35. Fearful, great God, from thine own sanctuaries!
        O God of Israël;
    He who doth give the people strength and power,
        O blessed be great God.

PSALM LXIX.

1.   Be saving me, great God,
For waters have come in to very soul!
2. I have been sinking into mire far down,
    Where is no standing-place:
I am come into deepnesses of waters,
Also the stream is sweeping me away.
3. I'm wearied while I call, my throat is hot;
Mine eyes are failing, hoping for my God.
4. More than the hairs upon my head abound
    My haters without cause;
Strong have grown they who are suppressing me,
    My wrongful enemies.
Although I robbed not, yet I must restore.
5. Great God, thou, thou hast known my foolishness;
Nor are my guiltinesses hid from thee.
6. Let not thy waiters be ashamed in me,
O Sovran Lord, Jehovah of the hosts;
Let not thy seekers be disgraced in me,
    O God of Israël.
7. For in thy cause I have endured reproach,
Disgrace hath been o'ercovering my face.
8. A stranger to my brethren I have been;
An alien also to my mother's sons.
9. For zeal of thine own house hath eaten me,
Reproach from thy reproachers fell on me.
10. When I will weep in fasting of my soul,
That will but bring reproaches down on me.
11. When for my clothing I put sackcloth on,
Then I became to them a ridicule.
12. A theme am I for sitters at the gate,
And for the songs of drunken levity.
13. Yet as for me, I crave from thee, Jehovah,

A time of favouring;
Great God, in thine own mercy manifold
O answer me in thy true saving grace.
14. O rescue me from clay; let me not sink;
I would be rescued from those hating me,
And also from the deepnesses of waters.
15. Let not the stream of waters sweep me off;
Nor let the shady deep down-swallow me;
Nor let the well shut over me its mouth.
16.   O answer me, Jehovah,
        For good thy mercy is:
In thy compassions great, O turn to me.
17. And from thy servant do not hide thy face;
For trouble hath me; haste to answer me.
18. Do thou come near my soul; O ransom it;
From these mine enemies redeem thou me.
19. Thou, thou hast known what have been my reproach,
Also my shame, and my dishonouring:
In front of thee are all my harassers.
20. Reproach hath broke my heart, and I am sick:
And though I wait for pity, there is none;
Also for comforters, none have I found.
21. But they will give in my refreshment gall,
And for my thirst make me drink vinegar.
22. Let their own table be a trap for them;
And their advantages become a snare.
23. Let their eyes darken that they may not see,
And cause their loins continually to slide.
24. Do thou pour on them thine indignant wrath,
And let thy furious anger seize on them.
25. Let their enclosure be made desolate;
Within their tents let there be none to sit.
26. For whom thou, thou didst smite, they have pursued;
And harshly of thy wounded ones they'll talk.

27. Put crookedness upon their crookedness,
    Nor let them come into thy righteousness.
28. Let them be blotted from the book of life;
    And with the righteous let them not be writ.
29. But as for me, afflicted and in pain,
    Thy saving grace, O God, will set me high.
30. I shall be praising God's name in a song,
    And magnifying him with thanksgiving.
31. This will more please Jehovah than an ox,
    A bullock horned and hoofed.
32.   The humble ones have seen;
    Glad shall be those inquiring after God,
        Also your hearts shall live.
33. Because Jehovah hears the needy ones,
    And he his prisoners hath not despised.
34. Him shall the heavens be praising, and the earth,
    The seas, and everything that moves in them.
35. For the great God will render Zion safe,
    And will be building Judah's cities up;
    And they shall sit there, as possessing her.
36. His servants' seed too shall inherit her,
    And lovers of his name shall dwell in her.

PSALM LXX.

1.   Great God, to rescue me,
    Jehovah, to my help do thou make haste.
2. They shall be put to shame and to dismay
        When seeking for my soul;
    They shall be turned backward and disgraced
        Delighting in my hurt.
3. They shall retreat on their own tracks of shame
        Who say Aha! Aha!

4. But shall be joyful, shall be glad in thee
        All those who seek for thee;
        Those shall say constantly,
        Let God be magnified,
Who are the lovers of thy saving grace.
5. And as for me, afflicted and in need,
        O God, make haste to me;
My helper and deliverer be thou;
        Jehovah, tarry not.

PSALM LXXI.

1. In thee, Jehovah, shelter I have sought:
O let me not be put to shame for aye.
2. Thou in thy righteousness wilt rescue me
        And cause me to escape:
Be thou inclining unto me thine ear,
        And be thou saving me.
3. Be thou for me a rocky dwelling-place
        Where I may go alway;
Thou hast commanded that I shall be saved,
Because my crag and fortalice art thou.
4. My God, deliver me from wicked hand,
From grasp of the unjust and cruel man.
5. For thou my expectation art, great Lord;
My confidence, Jehovah, from my youth.
6. On thee I've been upholden from my birth;
From mother's womb hast thou been rearing me;
In thee must be my praise continually.
7. A marvel I have been to multitudes,
But thou hast been my shelter-place of strength.
8. Filled shall my mouth be with the praise of thee;
All the day long with beauteousness of thee.

9. Cast me not off in season of old age;
    Like failing of my strength forsake me not.
10. For spoken have mine enemies at me;
    And my soul's watchers have consulting met,
11. Even to say, God hath forsaken him;
    Be ye pursuing, and be catching him
        When there's no rescuer.
12. Great God, do thou be not afar from me;
    My God, O to my help do thou make haste!
13. Let them be put to shame and wasting down,
        Opposers of my soul;
    Be covered with reproach and with disgrace
        The seekers of my hurt.
14. But as for me, I constantly will hope,
    And have been adding unto all thy praise.
15. My mouth shall oft declare thy righteousness;
    All the day long thy saving graciousness:
    Although I have not known the numberings.
16. I'll go through mighty acts of Lord Jehovah;
    I'll quote thy righteousness, yea, thine alone.
17. Thou, O great God, hast taught me from my youth.
    And up till now I'll show thy wondrous works:
18. Yet further till old age and hoary hairs,
    Great God, do thou be not forsaking me,
    Till I can show thine arm unto this race,
    To every coming one thy mightiness.
19. Thy righteousness, O God, high up doth reach,
    Thou who hast been the doer of great things;
    O thou great God, who can be like to thee?
20. Thou who hast made me see distressfulness,
        Full often and full sore,
    Wilt come, wilt quicken me again;
    And from the surging masses of the earth

Wilt come, wilt bring me up again.
21. Thou wilt give increase of my dignity;
And thou on every side wilt comfort me.
22. Then I, yea, I'll thank thee with psaltery,
The truth of thee, my God;
I shall be tuning psalms to thee with harp,
O Israel's holy One.
23. Sing brightly shall my lips,
While I tune psalms to thee;
This soul of mine too which thou hast redeemed.
24. Then too my tongue shall throughout all the day
Talk of thy righteousness;
For they are shamed, for they have been disgraced,
The seekers of my hurt.

PSALM LXXII.

1. GREAT God, thy judgements to the king give thou,
Thy righteousness unto the royal son.
2. He will redress thy folk with righteousness,
And thy afflicted ones with judgement just.
3. The mountains will bring peace unto the folk,
Also the little hills through righteousness.
4. He'll justly judge the afflicted of the folk,
He'll save the children of the needy one,
And break the oppressor down.
5. They shall fear thee while sun and moon endure
Through all the generations of mankind.
6. He shall come down like rain upon mown grass,
Like showers abundant watering the earth.
7. Flourish in his days shall the righteous man,
And plenteous peace until the moon shall fail.
8. And he shall overrule from sea to sea,

And from the river to the ends of earth.
9. Before his face shall crouch the desert tribes,
And enemies of him shall lick the dust.
10. The kings of Tarshish and of island shores
An offering shall bring back:
The kings of Sheba and of Seba shall
A goodly gift bring near.
11. To him shall worshipfully bow all kings;
The nations all shall service give to him.
12. For he'll outrid the needy one who cries,
The sufferer too when none is helping him.
13. He'll pity both the poor and needy one,
And souls of needy people he will save.
14. From fraud and violence he'll redeem their soul,
And precious will their blood be in his sight.
15. And he shall live,
And he will give to him of Sheba's gold,
And he will pray about him constantly:
All the day long he will be blessing him.
16. There shall a patch of corn be in the earth,
On top of mountains high;
Rustling like Lebanon shall be its fruit;
And they shall bloom from city
Like herbage of the earth.
17. The name of him shall be for evermore:
While sun endures his name shall still extend;
They'll bless themselves in him;
The nations all shall hail his happiness.
18. O blessed be Jehovah the great God,
The God of Israël,
Who doeth wondrous works, yea, he alone.
19. And blessed be his glorious name for aye;
And be his glory filling all the earth.
Amen, yea, and amen.

PSALM LXXIII.

1. Ah! good to Israel is the great God,
    To them whose heart is pure.
2. Yet as for me, almost my feet stretched off;
    Like nought my goings had been poured away.
3. For I was envying at boastful men;
    The peace of wicked men too I would see.
4. For there be no sore rigours at their death,
    And lusty is their frame.
5. In worry of frail mortals they are not;
    Nor are they stricken like as other men.
6. Therefore is pride become their necklacing,
    And violence a robe that covers them.
7. Their eye is standing out from fattiness;
    Excessive are the fancies of the heart.
8. They will insult, and will speak evilly;
    Oppression with a lofty tone they'll speak.
9. They've set into the heavens the mouth of them,
    Also their tongue will go about the earth.
10. Therefore his people hither shall return,
    And waters full shall be wrung out to them.
11. And they have said, How hath the Almighty known?
    Though knowledge must be in the One Most High.
12. Behold! these are the sons of wickedness;
    Yet prospering ever, they have grown in force.
13. Ah! 'tis in vain that I have cleansed my heart,
    And that I'll wash in innocence my hands.
14. And I am still a stricken one all day;
    And my reprovings come each morningtide.
15. If I have said, I will be talking thus,
    Lo! to thy race of sons I have proved false.
16. And while I think to know how this can be,
    It seems a grievous puzzle in my sight,

17. Until I go to sanctuaries of God;
And will consider of their latter end.
18. Ah! thou on slippery places wilt set them;
Thou hast made them fall down in total wreck.
19. How are they in a moment desolate!
They're ended, and can terrify no more.
20. Like dream at waking up, O Sovran Lord,
At rousing thou their image wilt despise.
21. Yet is my heart embittering itself,
And in my reins I sharply prick myself.
22. And I so brutish am, I will not know;
A very beast have I behaved with thee.
23. But yet I am continually with thee;
Thou hast been keeping hold of my right hand.
24. Thou by thy counsel wilt be leading me,
And afterwards wilt take me gloriously.
25.   Whom have I in the heavens?
And having thee I've no delight on earth.
26. Though failing hath my flesh been, and my heart,
The strong rock of my heart and portion is
      Great God for evermore.
27. For lo! those far from thee are perishing;
Thou hast supprest each one who whores from thee.
28.   But as for me,
The nearness of great God to me is good;
      And I have now
In Lord Jehovah set my shelter-place,
To give recount of all that thou hast done.

PSALM LXXIV.

1. O why, great God, hast thou off-spurned so long?
Why smokes thine anger at thy pastured sheep?
2. Think on thy company thou gat'st of old,

The ransomed rod of thine inheritance,
The hill of Zion whereon thou hast dwelt.
3. Be lifting up thy steps
Unto the utter ruins,
All broke by foemen in the holy mount.
4. Roared have thy harassers
In midst of thy set-place;
They have been putting up their signs for signs.
5. He shall be known as one who brings aloft
His hatchets on the thicket of the wood:
6. For now her open carvings one and all
With mallet and with chisel they will smash.
7. They've sent into the fire thy holy house;
Profaned to earth the dwelling of thy name.
8. They've said in heart, We'll maul them every one;
They've burnt all God's set-places in the land.
9. The signs we had we do no longer see;
There is no prophet now;
Nor is there with us one who knows how long.
10. How long, great God, shall troubler give reproach?
Shall enemy contemn thy name outright?
11. Why hold'st thou back thy hand, even thy right hand?
From midst thy bosom do thou make an end.
12. For the great God my King is from of old;
Working salvations in the midst of earth.
13. Thou, thou dividedst by thy strength the sea;
Didst shiver heads of dragons at the waters.
14. Thou, thou didst shatter heads of leviathan;
Didst make him food for folks of wilderness.
15. Thou, thou didst cleave the fountain and the stream;
Thou, thou didst dry the rivers of full flow.
16. Thine is the day; thine also is the night;
Thou, thou preparedst light-gift, and the sun.
17. Thou, thou hast firmed all borders of the earth;

Summer and winter, thou, thou formedst them.
18.   Remember this!
An enemy reproacheth, O Jehovah;
An impious people have contemned thy name.
19. Give not to greedy herd thy turtle-dove:
        Thine own afflicted flock
        Do thou not quite forget.
20.   Look to the covenant!
For filled are the dark places of the earth
        With homes of violence.
21. Let not the crusht one be again disgraced;
        Let weak and needy both
        Give praises to thy name.
22. Arise, great God! be pleading thine own cause;
Remember thy reproach from impious man
        Through all the day.
Forget not thou the voice of thy harassers;
        The voice of thine insurgents
        Which goes up constantly.

PSALM LXXV.

1. We have been rendering thanks to thee, great God;
We've rendered thanks; and that thy name is near
Hath been recounted by thy wondrous works.
2.   When I shall fix a time,
Then I, yea, I in uprightness will judge.
3. Dissolved is earth and all who dwell on it;
I, even I have meted its supports.   Selah.
4. I've said unto the boasters, Boast ye not:
And to the wicked, Raise ye not the horn;
5. Be not ye raising up your horn on high,
Nor speak ye with a neck of stubbornness.
6. For neither from sunrise nor from sundown,

Nor from the wilderness comes raising up;
7. But the great God is judge;
One he'll bring down, another he'll raise high.
8. Because a cup is in Jehovah's hand,
Whose wine is turbid, full of mingled stuff:
And he will pour from it.
Ah! to the dregs of it shall drain, shall drink
All wicked ones of earth.
9. But I, yea, I will manifest for aye,
I will be tuning psalms to Jacob's God.
10. All horns of wicked men I will cut off;
Upraised shall be the horns of righteous men.

PSALM LXXVI.

1. WELL known in Judah the great God hath been;
In Israël his name is magnified:
2. In Salem too will his pavilion be;
His habitation shall in Zion be.
3. There shivered He the firebolts of the bow,
The buckler, and the sword, and ranks of war. Selah.
4. Illustrious art thou!
More glorious than mountain heaps of prey.
5. A spoil they've made themselves, these stout of heart;
They're slumbering their sleep;
And none of all the men of valiantness
Had finding of their hands.
6. Because of thy rebuke, O Jacob's God,
Profoundly sleep both chariot and horse.
7. O thou, with reverence to be feared art thou,
And who can stand before the face of thee
When once thine anger moves?
8. From heaven thou hast made redress be heard;
The earth has been in fear and has been still,

9. When up arose for judgement the great God,
   So to be saving all the meek of earth.   Selah.
10. Surely the wrath of man shall give thee thanks,
    The residue of wraths thou wilt engird.
11.   Vow ye and well perform
    Unto Jehovah who is your own God;
         All who around him be
    Shall bring up presents to the Feared One.
12. He will snip out the spirit of high chiefs;
    Fearful is he unto the kings of earth.

PSALM LXXVII.

1. ALOUD to the great God I would cry out;
       Aloud to the great God,
       And he gave ear to me.
2.   In day of my distress
       The Sovran Lord I sought;
   My hand by night was run out ceaselessly,
   My soul refusing to be comforted.
3. Remembering God, I was disquieted;
   I would be musing, and my spirit sank.   Selah.
4. Thou didst keep hold on watches of mine eyes;
   My agitation would not let me speak.
5. I took to thinking on the days of old,
       The years of ages past;
6. Remembering my minstrelsy by night,
   Along with mine own heart then I would muse;
       My spirit would make search.
7. Is it for ever the great Lord will spurn?
   And will he not show favour any more?
8. Hath then his mercy ended utterly?
   Ceased hath the promise for each future age?
9. Hath mighty God forgotten to show grace?

      Or shut in anger his compassions up?   Selah.
10. But I will say, This is disease of mine,
     Misjudging the right hand of the Most High.
11. I will commemorate the deeds of Jah
     When minding from of old thy wondrousness;
12. When I have studied over all thy work,
     And on thy constant doings I will muse.
13. Great God, in holiness hath been thy way;
     What mighty one is truly great like God?
14. Thou, the Almighty, working wondrously,
     Thou hast made known among the folks thy strength.
15. Thou didst redeem with arm this folk of thine,
     The sons of Jacob, and of Joseph too.   Selah.
16. The waters seeing thee, O thou great God,
     The waters seeing thee, were quivering;
     Yea, also trembling were the surging deeps.
17. Down poured the waters from the murky clouds;
     A voice was being uttered from the skies;
     Yea, and thine arrows freely went about.
18. The voices of thy thunder rolled around;
     Bright flashed the lightning-bolts across the world;
     A trembling and a swaying seized the earth.
19.   Thy way is in the sea;
     And thy procedure is through waters vast;
     And the footprints of thee have not been known.
20. Thou led'st thy people like a flock of sheep
     Under the hand of Moses and Aaron.

PSALM LXXVIII.

1. Be giving ear, my people, to my law;
    Incline your ear to sayings of my mouth.
2. I'll open with a parable my mouth;
    Will freely tell the riddles of old time.

3. Things which we have been hearing, and will know,
   And which our fathers have declared to us,
4. We will not hide from their posterity;
   But to the coming race we will declare
   The praises of Jehovah and his strength,
   Also the wondrous doings which he wrought.
5. For he would raise a witnessing in Jacob,
   Also a law he set in Israël,
   Which he commanded that our forefathers
   Should make well known to their posterity;
6. In order that the coming race might know,
   And children yet unborn
   Might rise and tell to their posterity;
7. That they should put in God their confidence,
   And they should not forget the Almighty's deeds,
   But his commandment they should closely keep.
8. And they should not be as their fathers were,
   A race of stubborn and rebellious men,
   A race that did not firmly set its heart,
   Nor was their spirit faithful toward God.
9. The sons of Ephraim
   Though fully armed uplifters of the bow,
   Retired in day of conflict.
10. They did not keep the covenant of God,
    And in his law they did refuse to walk;
11. And were forgetful of his constant deeds,
    And wondrous works which he had made them see.
12. He in their fathers' sight wrought wondrously
    In land of Mizraim, the Zoan field.
13. He clave the sea, and caused them to pass through,
    And held the waters standing like a heap;
14. And he would lead them with a cloud by day,
    And all the night-time with a light of fire;
15. He would cleave rocks amid the wilderness,

And give them drink like depths abundantly.
16. And he would bring out flowing streams from crag,
And would make waters run down river-like.
17. But they would still be sinning against him;
Provoking the Most High in the dry land.
18. And they would tempt the Almighty in their heart,
Even to asking food they lusted for.
19. Moreover they would speak against great God;
They said, Can the Almighty One prevail
To spread a table 'mid the wilderness?
20. Behold! he smote the rock, and waters gushed,
And brooks would overflow;
But further is he able to give bread?
Can he make flesh-provision for his folk?
21. This when Jehovah heard, he would be wroth,
And fire was kindled against Jacob's sons,
And also anger rose at Israël,
22. Because they had not faith in the great God;
Nor were confiding in his saving grace.
23. Although he would command the skies above,
And doors of heaven he had open set,
24. And he would rain upon them manna food,
And corn of heaven he did give to them.
25. Bread of the mighty ones did each man eat;
Victual he sent to them sufficiently.
26. He would rouse up an east wind in the heavens,
And speed forth by his power a southern wind;
27. And he would rain like dust upon them flesh,
And like the sand of ocean, wingèd fowl.
28. And he would make these fall amid their camp
Around the very places where they dwelt:
29. So that they ate, and greatly were sufficed,
While their desire was being brought to them.
30. Not yet were they estranged from their desire;

Still was their food within the mouth of them,
31. When anger of great God rose up at them,
   And he would slay among their fatted ones,
   And Israel's choice young men he caused to bow.
32. Yet with all this they went on sinning still,
   And they believed not in his wondrous works.
33. So he would waste in vanity their days,
   Also their years in vext affrightedness.
34. Whene'er he slew them, they inquired for him,
   And they returned, and early sought for God.
35. They then would mind that great God was their Rock,
   And Mighty God, Most High, their ransomer.
36. Then they would speak him fairly with their mouth,
   And with their tongue would utter lies to him;
37. While yet their heart was not confirmed with him,
   Nor were they faithful with his covenant.
38. Yet he, so kind, would purge iniquity,
       And he would not destroy;
   Yea, many a time he drew his anger back,
   And would not stir up all his wrathfulness,
39. And would remember that but flesh were they;
   A breath that goeth, and will not return.
40. How oft would they provoke in wilderness!
   Would they be grieving him in desert land!
41. And would return and tempt the Almighty One,
   The Holy One of Israël they marked.
42. They did not keep in memory his hand,
   That day when he redeemed them from distress;
43. When he did set in Mizraim his signs,
   Also his miracles in Zoan's field;
44. And he would turn their rivers into blood,
   Also their flowing streams they could not drink;
45. Would send among them flies devouring them,
   As well as frogs to be corrupting them;

46. Would give to caterpillar their increase,
    Also their labour to the locust tribe;
47. He would kill down with heavy hail their vine;
    Also their sycomores with bitter frost;
48. And he would yield to heavy hail their beasts,
    Also their properties to fiery bolts;
49. He would send through them his great anger's heat,
    Fury, and indignation, and distress;
    A mission of the messengers of ills:
50. He would plan out a pathway for his anger;
    He kept not back from death the soul of them,
    And their live-stock to pestilence he yielded.
51. And he would smite all Mizraim's firstborn,
    Firstfruits of vigour in the tents of Ham.
52. Then would he rouse like flock of sheep his folk,
    And speed them drove-like into wilderness:
53. Would lead them safely, and they had no dread,
    While o'er their enemies the sea did close.
54. And he would bring them to his holy border,
    This mountain which his right hand hath acquired:
55. And he would drive out from before them nations,
    And make them fall through line of heritage;
    And cause to dwell within the tents of them
        The tribes of Israël.
56. Yet they would tempt, and they would disobey
        The great God, the Most High;
    His testimonies they would not observe:
57. But would be gone, and would act traitorously
        As their forefathers did:
    They had been turned like a deceitful bow:
58. And would provoke him with their high resorts,
    And make him jealous with their graven stocks.
59. The great God heard, and so he would be wroth,
    Rejecting Israël exceedingly;

60. And would forsake the Shiloh dwelling-place,
    The tent wherein he dwelt among mankind:
61. And would give to captivity his strength;
    Also his beauty into foeman's hand;
62. And would yield over to the sword his folk,
    And with his heritage he was full wroth.
63. Their choice young men the fire hath eaten up,
    Also their maids have not been held in praise.
64. Their priests by sword-stroke have been falling down;
    Also their widows will no weeping make.
65. Then woke, like one asleep, the Sovran Lord,
    Like mighty man exhilarate from wine;
66. And he would smite his harassers aback;
    Perpetual reproach he gave to them.
67. And he would be rejecting Joseph's tent,
    And tribe of Ephraim he did not choose,
68. But he would fix his choice with Judah's tribe,
    With this Mount Zion which indeed he loved.
69. And he would build right high his holy place;
    Like earth he founded it for evermore.
70. And he would choose in David his own servant,
    And would take him from foldings of the sheep,
71. From tending suckling ewes he brought him in
    To shepherdize o'er Jacob his own folk,
    And over Israël his heritage.
72. So he will feed them with a perfect heart,
    And will with skilful hands be leading them.

PSALM LXXIX.

1.   Great God,
   Heathens are come into thy heritage;
   They have defiled thy holy residence;
   Have laid Jerusalem in ruined heaps.

2. They have consigned thy servants' carcasses
    To be a food unto the fowls of heaven,
    Thy sainteds' flesh unto the beasts of earth.
3.   They've poured the blood of them
    Like waters round about Jerusalem,
            And none is burying.
4. We have been a reproach to dwellers here,
    A scorn and mock to those surrounding us.
5.   How long wilt thou, Jehovah,
            Be angry very sore?
    Will burn like as a fire thy jealousy?
6. Pour out thy wrath toward the heathen folks,
    Those who have had no knowledge of thyself;
            Upon those kingdoms too
    Which in the name of thee have made no call.
7. For they have been devouring Jacob up,
    Also his dwelling-ground they have laid waste.
8.   Remember not to us
            Iniquities bygone;
    Quickly let thy compassions come to us,
            For we're brought very low.
9. Help us, O thou our God of saving grace,
    In vindication of thy glorious name,
            And do thou rescue us;
    And make thou expiation of our sins
            For sake of thine own name.
10. Why is it that the heathen folks should say,
            Where is the God of these?
    Let there be known 'mong heathens to our sight
    Avengement of thy servants' poured-out blood.
11. Let come to thy regard the prisoner's groans;
            By greatness of thine arm
    Do thou reserve the sons of threatened death.
12. And give to our indwellers sevenfold

                Back to their breast,
    Reproach wherewith they have reproachèd thee,
                O Sovran Lord.
13.   But as for us,
    Who are thy people and thy pasture sheep,
    We will give thanks to thee for evermore:
                To generations all
    We will be telling forth the praise of thee.

PSALM LXXX.

1. SHEPHERD of Israël! do thou give ear:
        Guider of Joseph like a flock,
    Sitter between the cherubim, shine forth!
2.   In sight of Ephraim,
    In Benjamin's and in Manasseh's sight,
    Do thou be stirring up thy mightiness,
    And coming with thy saving help to us.
3.   Great God, be thou restoring us;
    Enlight thy face, and so we shall be saved.
4. O thou Jehovah, the great God of hosts,
            How long time hast thou smoked
            Against thy people's prayer!
5. Hast caused them to be eating bread of tears!
    And wilt thou make them drink of tears full cup?
6. Wilt thou set us a strife to dwellers here,
    And let our enemies be free to mock?
7. Great God of hosts, be thou restoring us;
    Enlight thy face, and so we shall be saved.
8. A vine from Mizraim thou wouldst remove,
    Wouldst drive out nations and wouldst plant in it.
9. Thou didst prepare before the face of it;
    And thou wouldst firmly root the roots of it,
            That it should fill the land.

10. O'ercovered were the mountains with its shade,
    And its great stems were cedar-trees of God.
11. It would send out its fruit-boughs to the sea,
    Also toward the river its young twigs.
12. Why hast thou battered its defences down?
    Till it gets pluckt by every passer-by:
13. Till it gets mangled by the forest boar,
    And creatures of the field will feed on it?
14. Great God of hosts, do thou return, we pray;
    Do thou be looking from the heavens, and see,
        And visit thou this vine:
15. And stablish what thine own right hand did plant,
    Even the son thou strengthenedst for thyself.
16. It hath been burnt with fire, it is cut down!
    From thy rebuking face they perish shall.
17. O let thy hand be on thy right-hand man,
    On son of man thou strengthenedst for thyself.
18. Then we shall not be turning off from thee;
    Thou'lt quicken us, and on thy name we'll call.
19. O thou Jehovah, the great God of hosts,
        Be thou restoring us:
    Enlight thy face, and so we shall be saved.

PSALM LXXXI.

1. O SING ye brightly to great God our strength!
   O shout ye loudly unto Jacob's God!
2. Lift up a psalm, and give the timbrel tune,
   The harp so pleasant with the psaltery.
3. Blow ye in new-moon time the trumpet-horn,
   In preparation of our festal day,
4. For a decree to Israël is this,
   A right pertaining unto Jacob's God;
5. This testimony he in Joseph set,

When he went out o'er land of Mizraim;
A lip whereof I knew not, I will hear.
6. I have removed his shoulder from the load;
His hands away from basket-work shall pass.
7. Thou in the strait didst call;
And I would pull thee out;
Would answer thee in thunder's secret place,
Would try thee at the waters Meribah. Selah.
8. Hear, O my folk; I'll witness against thee;
O Israël, do listen unto me;
9. Let there not be in thee a stranger god,
Nor bow thyself to worship heathen god.
10. I, even I, Jehovah, am thy God,
Who brought thee up from land of Mizraim;
Ope wide thy mouth, and I'll be filling it.
11. Yet did my folk not listen to my voice,
And Israël did not consent to me.
12. So I would send him forth
In hardness of their heart;
They shall go on in their own counsellings.
13. O if my folk were listening to me,
If Israël within my ways would walk,
14. Full quick their enemies I would subdue,
And on their troublers would turn back my hand.
15. Jehovah's haters should cringe down to him;
But their good season would be evermore.
16. And I would make him eat the fat of wheat,
And with rock-honey I would satiate thee.

PSALM LXXXII.

1. GREAT God doth stand in the divine assembly;
In midst of ruling gods he will be judging.

2. How long will ye be judging perversely?
　　And faces of the wicked will ye favour?　　　Selah.
3. Judge ye the case of poor and fatherless;
　　To sufferer and weak deal righteously.
4. Give ye escape for poor and needy one;
　　From hand of wicked men be rescuing.
5. They have not known, nor will they understand;
　　Through darkness they persist in walking on:
　　Moved will be all foundations of the earth.
6. I, I did say that ruling gods are ye,
　　And sons of the Most High are all of you.
7. But surely like as mankind ye shall die,
　　And like one of the princes ye shall fall.
8. Arise, great God! do thou be judging earth;
　　For thou, yea, thou art heir of nations all.

PSALM LXXXIII.

1. GREAT God, do not let silence be with thee;
　　Be thou not heedless; nor be still, O God.
2. For lo! thine enemies will make a stir;
　　Also thy haters have lift up the head.
3. Against thy folk they craftily will plot;
　　And will consult against thy close-kept ones.
4. They've said, Come, let us blot their nation out:
　　Let Israel's name be kept in mind no more.
5. For they've consulted with united heart;
　　Against thyself a covenant they will make.
6. The tents of Edom and the Ishmaelites,
　　　　Moab and Hagarenes,
7. Of Gebal, Ammon, and of Amalek,
　　Philistia with inhabitants of Tyre:
8. Also Assyria is joined with them;

       They've been an arm unto the sons of Lot.   Selah.
9. Do thou to them as unto Midian,
    As was to Sisera and Jabin done
        Beside the Kishon brook.
10. Destruction fell on them beside Endor;
    And they became but dung upon the ground.
11. Do thou be setting them, the chiefs of them,
        Like Oreb and like Zeeb;
    Also like Zebah and like Zalmunnah
        All royal ones of those
12. Who've said, Let us be taking for ourselves
        The pleasant homes of God.
13. My God, O set them like a rolling thing,
        Like stubble on the wind.
14.   As fire will burn a wood,
    And as a flame will set the hills ablaze,
15. Even so wilt thou pursue them with thy storm,
    And with thy tempest sorely trouble them.
16. Fill thou the faces of them with disgrace,
    That they may seek the name of thee, Jehovah.
17. They shall be shamed and troubled sore and long;
    Shall be dismayed, and shall be perishing.
18.   And men shall know that thou
    Thy name, Jehovah, even thou alone,
    Art the Most High One over all the earth.

PSALM LXXXIV.

1. O how belovèd is thy dwelling-place,
        Jehovah of the hosts!
2. Filled with desire, yea, fainting is my soul
        Toward Jehovah's courts;
    My very heart and flesh are crying out

Unto the living God.
3. (Even the sparrow hath obtained a house,
　　　The swallow hath her nest,
　Whereinto she hath laid her tender brood,)
　　　Thine altars to be near,
　　　Jehovah of the hosts,
　　　Who art my King and God.
4. O happy are the inmates of thy house;
　　　They still will give thee praise.　　　Selah.
5. O happy man who hath his strength in thee!
　　　The highways in their heart,
6. They as they journey on through Baca's vale
　　　A well-spring make of it:
　Yea, blessings will the early rain confer.
7. They shall be going on from force to force;
　Each shall appear in Zion before God.
8. O thou Jehovah, the great God of hosts,
　　　Be listening to my prayer;
　Do thou be giving ear, O Jacob's God.　　Selah.
9. Our shield do thou be seeing, O great God;
　And look on face of thine anointed One.
10. For better is a day in courts of thine
　　　Than thousand days;
　I'd rather keep a doorway in the house
　　　Of mine own God,
　Than dwell among the tents of wickedness.
11. 　　　For sun and shield hath been
　　　Jehovah the great God:
　Both grace and glory will Jehovah give:
　　　He will withhold no good
　　　From men of perfect walk.
12. 　　　Jehovah of the hosts,
　Happy the man who doth confide in thee.

PSALM LXXXV.

1. Thou wast well pleased, Jehovah, with thy land;
   Thou didst recall Jacob's captivity.
2. Thou didst remove thy folk's iniquity;
   Didst cover over all their sinfulness.   Selah.
3. Thou didst ingather all thy bursts of wrath;
   Thou didst withdraw thine anger from its heat.
4. Turn us again, our God of saving grace;
   And make thy provocation with us void.
5. Wilt thou for ever angry be at us?
   Or stretch thine anger out from age to age?
6. Wilt thou, yea, thou not quicken us again,
   That so thy people may be glad in thee?
7. Cause us to see thy mercy, O Jehovah,
   And thy salvation wilt thou give to us?
8. I will be listening what he will speak,
   The Almighty God Jehovah;
   For he'll be speaking peace unto his folk,
   And to his sainted ones;
   But let them not return to foolishness.
9. Ah! nigh his fearers his salvation is,
   That glory may be dwelling in our land.
10. Mercy and truth in company are met;
    Together righteousness and peace have kissed.
11. Now truth shall from the earth be springing up,
    And righteousness from heaven hath looked down.
12. Surely Jehovah will give what is good;
    Also our land will give productively.
13. Now righteousness before him will go on,
    And will be setting for a way his steps.

PSALM LXXXVI.

1. Incline thine ear, Jehovah, answer me;
   Because afflicted and in need am I.
2. Watch o'er my soul, for consecrate am I;
   O save thy servant; thou art God of me
      Who trustful look to thee.
3.   Show grace to me, O Lord,
   For unto thee I will call all the day.
4. Be thou engladdening thy servant's soul,
   For unto thee, O Lord, my soul I'll lift.
5. For thou, O Lord, art good and pardoning,
   And rich in mercy to all calling thee.
6. Be giving ear, Jehovah, to my prayer;
   Attend unto my supplicating voice.
7. In day of my distress I will call thee,
      For thou wilt answer me;
8. None is like thee among the gods, O Lord;
      And no works are like thine.
9. The nations all, which have been made by thee,
   Will come, and they in worship will bow down
      Before thy face, O Lord,
      And glorify thy name.
10. For great art thou, and doing wondrous works;
    Yea, thou thyself art God, and thou alone.
11. Point out to me, Jehovah, thine own way;
    I would be walking in thy truthfulness;
    Unite my heart to fearing of thy name.
12. I will give thanks to thee, O Lord my God,
       With all my heartiness;
    And I will glorify thy name for aye.
13. Because thy mercy hath been great to me;
       And thou hast pluckt my soul
       From Sheol's lower depth.

14. Great God, the proud have risen up at me,
    And crowd of cruel men have sought my soul,
    And they have not set thee in front of them.
15.   But thou, O Sovran Lord,
    A God compassionate and kind,
      Forbearing anger long,
    And rich in mercy and in truth,
16. Turn thou toward me, and show grace to me;
    Give thou thy strength to him who serveth thee;
    And be a Saviour to thy handmaid's son.
17. Do thou perform with me a sign for good;
    That so my haters seeing may be shamed,
      When thou, Jehovah, thou
    Hast been my helper and my comforter.

PSALM LXXXVII.

1. With his foundation on the holy hills,
2. Jehovah hath a love for Zion gates
    More than for Jacob's dwelling-places all.
3. Things glorious have been spoken about thee,
      O city of great God.   Selah.
4. I'll keep in mind Rahab and Babylon
      Among those knowing me:
    Behold! Philistia and Tyre, with Cush;
      This hath been born therein.
5. Also of Zion shall the saying be,
    This and that other man was born in her;
    And he will stablish her who is Most High.
6.   Jehovah will recount
      When peoples are writ up,
      This hath been born therein.   Selah.
7.   And they shall sing as well as pipe,
    My fountain-heads are all in thee.

PSALM LXXXVIII.

1. Jehovah, O my God of saving grace,
    By day I have cried out,
    By night in front of thee.
2. Into thy presence shall my prayer go;
    Do thou incline thine ear to mine outcry:
3. For satiate with ills hath been my soul,
    So that my life to Sheol they've drawn near.
4. Reckoned am I with goers down to pit:
    I have been like a man deprived of strength:
5.   Set free among the dead,
    Like as the slain ones lying in the grave,
    Those whom thou hast remembrance of no more,
    And they, they from thy hand have been cut off.
6. Thou hast put me into a pit far down,
    Into dark places, into shady deeps.
7. Upon me there hath leaned thy wrathfulness,
    And thou with all thy breakers didst afflict.   Selah.
8. Far thou hast put acquaintances from me;
    Hast made me utterly abhorred of them;
        Shut up, I can't go forth.
9. Mine eye is weakened through afflictedness;
    I have called thee, Jehovah, all the day;
    I have been stretching unto thee my hands.
10. Toward the dead wilt thou do wondrously?
    If the Rephaim rise, will they thank thee?   Selah.
11. Shall in the grave thy mercy be declared?
    Thy faithfulness in the destroyer's realm?
12. Shall in the dark thy wondrousness be known,
    And in oblivion's land thy righteousness?
13.   But as for me,
    I have to thee, Jehovah, cried for help;
    And every morn my prayer before thee goes.

14. Why, O Jehovah, wilt thou spurn my soul?
    Wilt thou be keeping hid thy face from me?
15. Afflicted and at death's door from my youth,
    I've borne thy terrors; I am ill at ease.
16. Upon me there have passed thy heated wraths;
    Thy dread alarms have been suppressing me.
17. They've compassed me like waters all the day;
    They have closed in upon me all at once.
18. Far thou hast put from me lover and friend,
    Acquaintances of mine are darkness.

PSALM LXXXIX.

1. JEHOVAH's mercies I will ever sing;
       To generations all
   My mouth shall make thy faithfulness be known.
2.   For I have said,
   Eternally shall mercy be built up;
       The heavens high,
   Thou wilt confirm thy faithfulness in them.
3. I've made a covenant to my chosen one,
   To David mine own servant I have sworn;
4. Till evermore I will confirm thy seed,
   And I have built to generations all
       The throne of thee.   Selah.
5. And heaven shall praise thy wondrousness, Jehovah,
       Yea, and thy faithfulness
   In the assembly of the holy ones.
6. For who in sky may with Jehovah rank?
   May like Jehovah be, 'mong sons of might?
7.   A God most terrible
   Amid the council of the holy ones,
   And feared above all those surrounding him!
8. O thou Jehovah, the great God of hosts,

Who is there like as thou, the Strong One, Jah?
Also thy faithfulness surrounding thee?
9. Thou ruling o'er the swelling of the sea;
When heave its billows, thou, thou stillest them.
10. 'Twas thou who crushedst Rahab like one slain;
With thy strong arm thou scatteredst thy foes.
11. Thine are the heavens, yea, thine is the earth;
The world and fulness thereof thou didst found.
12. The north and south, thou, thou createdst them;
Tabor and Hermon in thy name will shout.
13. To thee belongs an arm of mightiness;
Strong is thy hand, exalted thy right hand.
14. Justice and judgement keeping firm thy throne,
Mercy and truth shall be before thy face.
15. Happy the folk who know the joyful sound;
Jehovah, in thy face-light they shall walk.
16. In thy name they rejoice shall all the day,
And in thy righteousness shall be upraised.
17. Because the beauty of their strength art thou;
And through thy favour shall be raised our horn.
18. For to Jehovah doth belong our shield,
Also to Israel's Holy One our king.
19. Then thou didst speak in vision to thy saint,
   And thou wouldst say,
I have laid fitting help on one of might;
I have upraised one chosen from the people.
20. I have found David mine own servant out;
Have with my holy oil anointed him:
21. That so my hand may be confirmed with him,
Moreover that mine arm may strengthen him.
22. Ne'er shall an enemy exact from him,
Nor son of wrongfulness be humbling him.
23. And I have beat his troublers from his face,
And those who are his haters I will smite.

24. My faithfulness and mercy are with him,
    And in my name shall be upraised his horn.
25. And I have set into the sea his hand,
    Also into the rivers his right hand.
26. He, he will call me, thou my Father art,
    Mine own God, and my rock of saving help.
27. Moreover I will give him as firstborn,
    As the Most High One to the kings of earth.
28. For ever I will keep to him my mercy,
    Also my covenant stedfastly to him.
29. And I have set for evermore his seed,
    Also his throne like as the days of heaven.
30. But if his children will forsake my law,
    And in my judgements they will not go on;
31. If they my statutes will profanely break,
    And my commandments they will not observe,
32. Then visit I with rod their trespasses,
    And with sore smitings their iniquity.
33. But I my mercy wont make void from him,
    Nor will I falter in my faithfulness.
34. I never will profane my covenant,
    The outflow of my lips I will not change.
35. One thing I've sworn to in my holiness;
    Assuredly to David I'll not lie:
36. His seed unto eternity shall be,
    His throne too, like the sun in front of me;
37. Like as the moon shall be confirmed for aye,
    And be a stedfast witness in the sky.   Selah.
38. Yet thou, O thou hast spurned, and wilt reject;
    Thou hast waxt wroth with thine anointed one;
39. Thou hast broke through thy servant's covenant;
    Hast been profaning to the earth his crown.
40. Thou hast down-battered his defences all;
    Hast made his strongholds to be ruinous.

41. He is despoiled by every passer-by;
    He hath been a reproach to dwellers here.
42. Thou hast upraised the right hand of his troublers;
    Thou hast made gladsome all his enemies.
43. Yea, thou'lt withdraw the vigour of his sword;
    And hast not made him rise in battle's brunt.
44. Thou hast wrought ceasing of his brilliancy;
    Also his throne thou to the earth hast hurled.
45. Thou hast cut short the daytime of his youth;
    Hast caused him to be covered o'er with shame.   Selah.
46. How long, Jehovah, wilt thou hide thee quite?
    Will burn like as a fire thy wrathfulness?
47. Remember as to me, what lifetime is!
        O'er how much hollowness
    Thou hast created all the sons of men!
48.   What man shall be in life
        And not be seeing death?
    Shall he keep free his soul from Sheol's hand?   Selah.
49.   Where may thy mercies be,
        The former ones, O Lord,
    As sworn to David in thy faithfulness?
50.   Remember thou, O Lord,
        Reproaching of thy servants;
        My bearing in my bosom
        All peoples manifold;
51. Whom have reproached thine enemies, Jehovah,
        When they've reproached the steps
        Of thine anointed one.
52. Blest be Jehovah to eternity;
        Amen, yea, and amen.

PSALM XC.

1. O Sovran Lord, a habitation thou
   Hast been for us in generations all.
2. Even before the mountains were brought forth,
   Or thou wast fashioning the earth and world,
   Both from and to the far eternities
      Art thou, O God.
3. Thou wilt turn back frail man to very dust;
   And thou wilt say, Return, ye sons of men.
4. Whereas a thousand years may in thy sight
   Be as a day, a passing yesterday,
   Or even as a watch-time in the night.
5. Thou hast down-poured them; sleeping they will be
   At morning like the grass, there comes a change.
6. At morning it will blossom, and hath changed:
   At evening it is mown, and withereth.
7. So we've been wasting in thine angriness;
   And in thy wrath we have been troubled sore.
8. Thou didst put our misdeeds in front of thee,
   Our secret sins in light of thine own face.
9.   So all these days of ours
       Are turned off in thy rage:
   We have consumed our years like as a moan
10.   The days of these our years,
        They are but seventy years:
       And if through mightiness
        They may be eighty years,
    Yet is their stoutness toil and vanity,
    For quick the time draws on when we must fly.
11. Who doth well know thine anger's energy?
    And in proportion to thy fear thy rage.
12. To count our days do thou make known aright,

That we may bring a heart of wisdom in.
13. Do thou return, Jehovah; O how long!
And pity on thy servants do thou take.
14. O satisfy us early with thy mercy,
That we may brightly sing, and may be glad
Through all these days of ours.
15. Englad us like the days thou humbledst us,
The years we have been seeing evil in.
16. Display unto thy servants thine own work,
Also thine excellence upon their sons.
17.   And let there be on us
The beauty of Jehovah our own God;
And work of our own hands
Do thou confirm on us:
Yea, work of our own hands, confirm thou it.

PSALM XCI.

1. To sit in secret place of the Most High,
Is in the Almighty's shade to lodge oneself.
2.   I'll to Jehovah say,
My shelter and my fort,
My God, I will be putting trust in him.
3.   Because that he,
He will deliver thee from fowler's trap,
From pestilence of crimes.
4. He with his pinions will o'ercover thee;
And underneath his wings thou'lt shelter find;
A buckler and protector is his truth.
5. Thou shalt not fear for terror of the night,
Nor for the arrow that may fly by day;
6. For pestilence that may in darkness walk,
Nor for destruction that may waste at noon.
7. Though there may fall a thousand at thy side,

>   Even a myriad at thy right hand,
>   Near thee it shall not come.
> 8. But only with thine eyes thou shalt look on,
>   And the reward of wicked men shalt see,
> 9.   Since that thou hast
>   Jehovah, mine own shelter, the Most High,
>   Thy habitation made;
> 10. There shall not happen to thee aught of ill,
>   Nor shall a stroke find entrance to thy tent.
> 11. For he will charge his angels as to thee,
>   To keep thee watchfully in all thy ways;
> 12. Upon their hands shall they be bearing thee
>   Lest that thou hit thy foot against a stone.
> 13. On jackal and on serpent thou shalt tread;
>   Shalt tramp the lion and the dragon down.
> 14. Since he in me delights, I'll rescue him;
>   I'll set him high because he knows my name.
> 15. He will call me, and I will answer him;
>   Along with him shall I be in distress;
>   I'll pull him through, and I will honour him.
> 16. With length of days I will him satisfy,
>   And will cause him to see my saving grace.

PSALM XCII.

> 1. It is good to give thanks to Jehovah;
>   And to tune of thy name, O Most High.
> 2. To show forth in the morning thy mercy,
>   And thy faithfulness every night,
> 3. On a ten-stringed lyre and a psaltery,
>   In a soft solemn strain with the harp.
> 4. For thou'st gladdened me, Lord, with thy doing;
>   Of thy handworks I'll joyfully sing.
> 5. O how great have thy works been, Jehovah!
>   Very deep have thy projectings been.

6. A mere brutish man will not have knowledge,
   Nor a fool have discernment of this.
7. When the wicked grow up like the herbage,
   Though may bloom all the doers of wrong,
   It is toward their lasting destruction.
8.   Whereas thou, O Most High,
     Art for ever, Jehovah.
9. For thine enemies, lo! O Jehovah,
   For thine enemies, lo! they shall perish;
   All the doers of wrong shall disperse.
10. But thou'lt raise high my horn like the bison's;
    I am instinct with verdurous oil.
11. And mine eye shall look through mine observers;
    When evil men rise up against me,
      Mine ears shall o'erhear.
12. He who's righteous shall grow like the palm-tree;
    Like a Lebanon cedar he'll spread.
13. Those implanted in house of Jehovah
    In the courts of our God shall make growth.
14. They shall still give increase when grey-headed;
    They in fatness and verdure shall be;
15. To show that upright is Jehovah,
    My strong rock; and no flaw is in him.

PSALM XCIII.

1. JEHOVAH reigns, in majesty is clothed;
   Clothed is Jehovah, self-begirt with strength:
   Yea, fixt will be the earth immovably.
2. Firm fixt hath been thy throne from olden time;
     From evermore art thou.
3. The rivers, O Jehovah, have lift up,
   The rivers have been lifting up their voice,
   The rivers will be lifting up their spray.
4. More than the voice of waters manifold,

Or of sublimest breakers of the sea,
Sublime in loftiness Jehovah is.

5. Thy testimonies are exceeding sure:
For thine own house most fit is holiness,
Jehovah, through the long extent of days.

PSALM XCIV.

1. ALMIGHTY God of vengeances, Jehovah,
Almighty God of vengeances, shine forth,
2. Do thou lift up thyself, O Judge of earth;
Return a recompense upon the proud.
3. How long, Jehovah, shall the wicked men,
How long shall wicked men be triumphing?
4. They will be talking fast, will speak hard things,
They will be boastful, all these wrongdoers.
5. Thy people, O Jehovah, they will crush;
And thine inheritance they will afflict.
6. The widow and the sojourner they'll slay;
The orphans too they will be murdering.
7. And they'll be saying, Jah shall never see,
Nor shall the God of Jacob understand.
8. O understand, ye brutish of the folk;
And, O ye fools, when will you wisely act?
9. The planter of the ear, shall he not hear?
If former of the eye, shall he not look?
10. Warner of nations, shall he not reprove?
He who is teaching mankind what to know,
11. Jehovah knows the projects of mankind,
That these are vanity.
12.   O happy is the man
He whom thou wilt be chastening, O Jah,
And from thy law thou wilt be teaching him,
13. To give him quietness from evil days,

Till for the wicked man be dug a pit.
14. Because Jehovah will not leave his folk,
    Nor his inheritance will he forsake,
15. But back to righteousness shall judgement turn,
    And in its train all those of upright heart.
16. Who will arise with me against ill men?
    Who will stand by me against wrongdoers.
17. Had not Jehovah been a help to me,
    Soon would my soul have dwelt in silentness.
18. Though I did say, My foot was moving off,
    Thy mercy, O Jehovah, holds me up.
19. When crowding cares are in the midst of me,
    Thy consolations will delight my soul.
20. Can there accord with thee a throne of crimes,
    Which frameth mischief by a statute-law?
21. They'll muster forth against a righteous soul,
    And blood of guiltless one they will condemn.
22. Yet will Jehovah be my safe high place;
    Also my God shall be my shelter-rock.
23. He will back-turn upon themselves their strength
    And in their evilness will them suppress;
    Suppress them will Jehovah our own God.

PSALM XCV.

1. O come, let us sing gladly to Jehovah!
   Make shouting to our God of saving help!
2. Let us approach his presence with thanksgiving,
   With tuneful psalming let us shout to him!
3. Because a God of greatness is Jehovah;
   Also a King great over all the gods.
4. Who in his hand retains the earth's recesses;
   Also the piling heights of hills are his.
5. To him belongs the sea, for he, he made it;

Also the dry land which his hands did form.
6. Come in! let us be worshipping and bending,
Kneeling before Jehovah our Creator,
7.   For he is our own God;
And we, we are the people of his pasture
           And sheep-flock of his hand.
To-day, if ye unto his voice will listen,
8. O harden not your hearts like Meribah,
Like day of Massah in the wilderness;
9. What time your forefathers were tempting me,
They did me try; yea, and they saw my deed.
10. Through forty years I grieved about that race,
And said, a folk of straying heart are they;
And they, no knowledge have they of my ways:
11. Of whom I have been saying in mine anger,
That they shall not find entrance to my rest.

PSALM XCVI.

1. O SING ye to Jehovah a new song!
O sing ye to Jehovah, all the earth!
2. O sing ye to Jehovah, bless his name!
Proclaim from day to day his saving grace.
3. Tell to the nations what his glory is;
To all the peoples what his wonders are.
4. For great's Jehovah, and supremely praised;
Fearful hath he been above all the gods.
5. For all gods of the peoples are but dolts;
Whereas Jehovah, he the heavens did make.
6. Honour and majesty before him are;
With strength and beauty in his holy place.
7. Give to Jehovah, O ye clans of peoples,
Give to Jehovah gloriousness and strength.

8. Give to Jehovah glory of his name;
   Bring ye a gift, and come into his courts.
9. O bow ye worshipfully to Jehovah
            In beauty of holiness.
   Be quivering at his presence, all the earth.
10. Say ye 'mong nations that Jehovah reigns;
    Yea, fixt shall be the world immovably;
    He will redress the peoples uprightly.
11.   The heavens shall be glad,
            The earth too shall rejoice,
    The sea and fulness thereof shall resound;
12. The field and all that's in it shall exult;
    Then shall all trees of forest brightly sing,
13. In presence of Jehovah; for he comes,
    For he hath come to be the judge of earth.
    And he will judge the world in righteousness,
    Also the peoples in his faithfulness.

PSALM XCVII.

1. JEHOVAH reigneth; let the earth rejoice!
   And let the many sea-girt lands be glad!
2. A cloud and awful gloom around him are;
   Justice and judgement keeping firm his throne.
3. A fire before his presence will move on,
   And will be flaming round his harassers.
4. Brightly have flashed his lightnings o'er the world;
   The earth has seen, and will be quivering.
5. The mountains have like wax been melted down
            Before Jehovah's face;
   Before the Sovran Lord of all the earth.
6. The heavens have displayed his righteousness,
   And peoples all have seen his gloriousness.

7. Shamed shall be all who serve a graven stock;
   They who do boast themselves in idol dolts;
   Bow down to him in worship, all ye gods.
8. Zion hath heard, and gladsome she will be;
   Also the Judah daughters will rejoice
   By reason of thy judgements, O Jehovah.
9.   Because, Jehovah, thou
   Art the Most High One over all the earth,
   Greatly exalted above all the gods.
10. O lovers of Jehovah, hate ye ill;
    He watching o'er his sainted people's souls
    From hand of wicked men will rescue them.
11. There is a light sown for the righteous man,
    And for straightforward hearts there's gladsomeness.
12. Be gladsome, O ye righteous, in Jehovah,
    And thankful when ye mind his holiness.

PSALM XCVIII.

1. O SING ye to Jehovah a new song!
     For wonders he hath done;
   He victory hath got by his right hand
     And by his holy arm.
2. Jehovah hath made known his saving help,
     To eyes of Gentile folks
     Hath proved his righteousness;
3. Did mind his mercy and his faithfulness
     To house of Israël;
   All the far endings of the earth have seen
   The saving helpfulness of our own God.
4. Shout ye unto Jehovah, all the earth;
   Break forth, and brightly sing, and tune the psalm.
5. Tune psalms unto Jehovah with the harp,
   With harp and with a voice of melody:

6. With trumpeting and with the cornet's voice,
    Do ye shout out before
    The King Jehovah's face.
7. The sea and fulness thereof shall resound;
    The world and the inhabitants therein.
8. The rivers shall be clapping with the hand;
    Together shall the mountains brightly sing
9.   Before Jehovah's face;
    For he hath come to be the judge of earth;
    And he will judge the world in righteousness,
    Also the peoples in straightforwardness.

PSALM XCIX.

1. JEHOVAH reigneth; peoples tremble shall;
    He sits between the cherubs; earth shall move.
2. Jehovah amid Zion hath been great;
    And raised is he above the peoples all.
3. They'll thank thy name as great and to be feared;
    The Holy One is he.
4. Also the kingly strength did judgement love;
    Thou, thou didst firmly settle equity;
    Judgement and righteousness 'mong Jacob's folk
        Hast thou, yea, thou wrought out.
5. Do ye exalt Jehovah our own God;
    And bow in worship at footstool of Him;
    The Holy One is he.
6. Moses and Aäron among his priests;
    And Samuel with them who call his name;
        These calling to Jehovah,
        He, he would answer them.
7. In cloudy pillar he would speak to them;
    They did observe his testimonies,
    And statute he did give to them.

8.   Jehovah our own God,
    Thou, thou didst answer them.
  A God of pardon thou hast been to them,
  Yet taking vengeance on their practices.
9. Do ye exalt Jehovah our own God;
  And bow in worship at his holy hill,
  For holy is Jehovah our own God.

PSALM C.

1. Shout ye unto Jehovah, all the earth!
2. Do service to Jehovah gladsomely:
  Come ye before his face with joyful song.
3. Know that Jehovah, he is the great God;
  'Twas he who made us, and not we ourselves,
  To be his people and his pasture-sheep.
4. Come ye into his gates with thanksgiving,
  Into his courts with offering of praise.
  Give thanks to him; O do ye bless his name.
5.   For good Jehovah is;
    His mercy lasts for aye,
    And unto ages all
    His faithfulness extends.

PSALM CI.

1. Of mercy and of judgement I will sing:
  To thee, Jehovah, I will tune the psalm.
2. I will act wisely in a perfect way.
    When wilt thou come to me?
  I will be walking with a perfect heart
    In midst of mine own house.
3. I shall not set in front of mine own eyes
    A thing of Belial;

The working of apostasies I hate;
    It shall not cling to me.
4. A heart perverted shall depart from me;
    Evil I will not know;
5. One slandering his neighbour privily,
    Even him I will suppress;
 A man of lofty eyes and selfish heart,
    Him I shall not endure.
6. Mine eyes are on the faithful of the earth
    That they may sit with me;
 He who is walking in a perfect way
    Shall be my minister.
7. There shall not sit in midst of mine own house
    One working guilefully:
    One given to speaking false,
 Shall have no settlement before mine eyes.
8.   Each morn I will suppress
    All wicked of the land,
 To cut from off the city of Jehovah
    Ungodly doers all.

PSALM CII.

1. JEHOVAH, do thou listen to my prayer;
 And let my cry for help go in to thee.
2. Do not be keeping hid thy face from me
    In day of my distress:
 Be thou inclining unto me thine ear;
 What day I call, O quickly answer me.
3. For wasting into smoke have been my days,
 Also my bones like burning brands are hot.
4. Smit like the herb, my heart is drying up,
 Because I have forgot to eat my bread.
5.   Through loudness of my sighs

My bone is clinging fast unto my flesh.
6. I'm deemed like pelican of wilderness;
   I have been as an owl of ruined wastes;
7. I have watched wakefully, till I shall be
   Like little bird alone upon housetop.
8. All day mine enemies have me reproached,
   Infatuate men against me have made oath.
9. Since ashes like as bread I have been eating,
   Also my drink with weeping I have mingled,
10. Beneath thine indignation and thy wrath,
    For thou hast lift me, and wilt cast me forth.
11. My days are like a shadow far stretcht out;
    And I, like herbage I shall be dried up.
12. But thou, Jehovah, thou for aye wilt sit,
    And thy memorial be to ages all.
13. Thou, thou wilt rise, wilt love to Zion show,
      When time to favour her,
      When the set time is come;
14. When pleased have been thy servants with her stones,
    And to her dust they will act graciously.
15. And nations will revere Jehovah's name,
    And all the kings of earth thy gloriousness.
16. What time Jehovah builded Zion up
      His gloriousness was seen.
17. He turned toward the prayer of destitute,
    And he did not despise the prayer of them.
18. This shall be written for a future race,
    And folk to be created shall praise Jah.
19. For he looked downward from his holy height;
      Jehovah out of heaven
      Unto the earth did gaze,
20. To hear the groaning of the prisoner,
    To liberate the sons of threatened death;
21. To tell in Zion of Jehovah's name,

And of his praises in Jerusalem,
22. When gathered shall the folks together be,
And kingdoms to do service to Jehovah.
23. He hath afflicted in the way my strength,
He hath cut short my days.
24. I will say, O my God,
Take me not up in mid-time of my days.
Throughout all generations are thy years.
25. In early time the earth thou diddest found;
Also thy handiwork the heavens were.
26. They, they shall perish, but thou, thou shalt stand:
Yea, all of them like garment shall wear out;
Like vesture thou wilt cause them to be changed,
And they shall changèd be.
27. But thou shalt be the same,
And thine own years can never have an end.
28. Sons of thy servants shall have dwelling-place,
Their seed too in thy presence shall be staid.

PSALM CIII.

1. GIVE blessing to Jehovah, O my soul;
And all within me, bless his holy name.
2. Give blessing to Jehovah, O my soul,
Nor be forgetting all his benefits.
3. Who pardoneth all thine iniquities;
Who healeth all thy sore diseasedness;
4. Who is redeeming from the pit thy life;
Who crowneth thee with mercy and fond love;
5. Who satisfies with real good thy soul;
And thou renewest eagle-like thy youth.
6. Outworking righteousness Jehovah is;
And judgements for all them who are opprest.
7. He would make known to Moses his own ways,

To sons of Israël his constant deeds.
8. Compassionate and kind Jehovah is,
To anger slow, in mercy plentiful.
9. Not to extremity will he contend;
And not for ever will he bear a grudge.
10. Not like our sinning hath he done to us,
Nor like our guilt hath he rewarded us.
11. For like the height of heaven o'er the earth,
Strong is his mercy o'er his fearing ones.
12. Like to the farness of the east from west,
Hath he put far from us our trespasses.
13. Like as a father o'er his children yearns,
So yearns Jehovah o'er his fearing ones.
14. For he, yea, he hath known the frame of us,
Keeping in mind that only dust are we.
15. Frail man! like to the grass have been his days;
Like blooming of the field, so he shall bloom.
16. For through him goes a breath, and he is not;
And no more shall his place acknowledge him.
17. Yet hath Jehovah's mercies ever been,
And ever shall be on his fearing ones;
Also his righteousness to sons of sons,
18. To those who keep his covenant, and those
Who mind his precepts to be doing them.
19. Jehovah hath in heaven fixt his throne,
And he as king o'er everything doth rule.
20. O bless Jehovah, ye his messengers,
Mighty in strength, the doers of his word;
Eager to catch the voices of his word.
21. Give blessing to Jehovah, all his hosts,
His ministers, the doers of his will:
22. Give blessing to Jehovah, all his works,
In all the places of his Sovran rule:
Give blessing to Jehovah, O my soul.

PSALM CIV.

1. Give blessing to Jehovah, O my soul!
   Jehovah, thou, my God, art very great;
   With honour and with majesty art clothed.
2. Covering thyself with light as with a robe
   Stretching afar the heavens curtain-like.
3. Who lays in waters his high-chamber beams,
   Who takes the thick clouds for his chariot;
   Who moves along upon the wings of wind.
4. Who makes his messengers to be the winds;
   His ministers to be the flaming fire.
5. He founded earth upon its settlements,
   That it should not be moved for evermore.
6. With surging deep, like clothes, thou cover'dst it;
   Above the mountains would the waters stand.
7. From thy rebuking they would flee away;
   From thy loud thunder they would hasten off.
8. They'll go up mountains; they will go down vales,
   Unto the place which thou didst found for them.
9. A mark thou gavest which they should not pass,
   Nor turn again to cover up the earth.
10. He sendeth springs into the river-dales;
    Between the mountains they will flow along.
11. They will give drink to all the beasts of field;
    Wild asses will assuage their thirstiness.
12. Above them will the fowls of heaven dwell,
    From 'mid the leafage giving forth their voice.
13. He slakes the mountains from his lofty halls;
    By thy works' fruit the earth is satisfied.
14. He causeth grass to spring for herd and flock;
    And herbage for the husbandry of man,
    For bringing out provision from the earth:
15. And wine shall glad the heart of feeble man,

To make his visage glisten more than oil,
And bread shall mankind's feeble heart uphold.
16. Well satisfied shall be Jehovah's trees;
Cedars of Lebanon which he did plant;
17. Wherein the little birds will build their nests;
As for the stork, the fir-trees are her home.
18. The lofty mountains are the wild goats' haunt;
The crags are for the shaphan's sheltering.
19. He made the moon to mark appointed times;
The sun hath known his when and where to set.
20. Thou wilt bring darkness and there shall be night,
In which all forest-life will move about;
21. The younger lions roaring for the prey,
And for the seeking of their food from God.
22. The sun will rise; they will be gathered up;
And in their several haunts they will lie down.
23. Man will go forth unto his handicraft,
And to his husbandry till eventide.
24. How manifold, Jehovah, are thy works!
The whole of them in wisdom thou hast wrought;
Filled has the earth been with thy properties.
25. This too, the sea, both large and widely spread,
Therein are moving things innumerable,
Creatures alive, both small and great of bulk.
26. There will the ships be going to and fro;
Leviathan,
This thou hast formed for making play therein.
27. They all of them to thee will eager look
For giving of their food in season due.
28. Thou wilt give out to them, they will pick up:
Thou'lt ope thy hand; they are sufficed with good.
29. Thou'lt hide thy face, they will be troubled sore;
Thou'lt gather in their breath, they will expire;
And back unto their dust they shall return.

30. Thou'lt send thy breath, created they shall be:
    And thou'lt renew the surface of the ground.
31. Jehovah's glory shall be evermore;
    Glad shall Jehovah be in his own works:
32. He who doth look at earth, and it shall quake;
    He may but touch the hills, and they shall smoke.
33. I'll sing unto Jehovah while I live;
    I'll tune to my God while my being lasts.
34. Sweet may my meditation be of him;
    May I, yea, I be gladsome in Jehovah.
35. May sinners be extinguisht from the earth;
    And wicked men, may they no longer be.
    Give blessing to Jehovah, O my soul.
          O praise ye Jah!

PSALM CV.

1. THANK ye Jehovah, call upon his name;
   Make known among the folks his constant deeds.
2. Sing ye to him, be tuning unto him;
   Talk thoughtfully of all his wondrous works.
3. O do ye glory in his holy name;
   Glad be the heart of them who seek Jehovah.
4. Inquire ye for Jehovah and his strength;
   O do ye seek his face continually.
5. Keep ye in mind the wonders which he wrought,
   His marvels and the judgements of his mouth.
6. O seed of Abraham, his servant true,
   Ye sons of Jacob, his own chosen ones.
7. 'Tis he who is Jehovah our own God;
   Throughout the whole of earth his judgements are.
8. He keeps in mind for aye his covenant,
   A word ordained to thousand generations;
9. That which he ratified with Abraham,

Also the oath which he to Isaac sware;
10. Confirming it to Jacob for a law,
To Israël a covenant for aye.
11. Saying, I unto thee will give the land,
Canaan, the portion of your heritage;
12. While they were yet in number very few,
A little band, and sojourners therein.
13. While they would go from nation unto nation;
Out from a kingdom to another folk;
14. He suffered none to be oppressing them,
But for their sakes would be reproving kings.
15. Lay not your touch on mine anointed ones,
Nor to my prophets do ye any harm.
16. Then he would call a famine on the land;
The universal staff of bread he brake.
17. He sent to be their forerunner a man;
Away to servitude was Joseph sold.
18. They put the galling fetters on his feet;
Into the iron had his soul to go.
19. Until the timely coming of his word,
Jehovah's saying was refining him.
20. The king did send, and would unfetter him;
Ruler of peoples, he would loosen him.
21. He set him to be lord of his own house,
And ruler over all his properties,
22. To bind his princes to his own intent;
Also his senators he would make wise.
23. Then Israël went into Mizraim,
And Jacob sojourned in the land of Ham.
24. And he would greatly fructify his folk,
And make them stronger than their harassers.
25. He turned the heart of these to hate his folk,
To deal against his servants craftily.
26. He sent forth Moses who was serving him,

Aaron whom also he had chosen out;
27. These set among them his authentic signs,
    Also his marvels in the land of Ham.
28. He sent forth darkness, and would make it dark,
    And they were not rebellious to his word.
29. He turned the waters for them into blood,
    He also caused the fish therein to die.
30. Their land produced great multitudes of frogs,
    Into the private chambers of their kings.
31. He said, and then would enter in the fly,
    The lice throughout the whole of their domain.
32. He gave their heavy showers in form of hail,
    A fire of flashing flames throughout their land.
33. And he would smite their vines and their fig-trees,
    And break the timber growth of their domain.
34. He said, and then would come the locust swarm
    And cankerworm beyond a reckoning.
35. And it would eat all herbage in their land,
    And it would eat the fruitage of their soil.
36. Then he would smite all firstborn in their land,
    Firstfruits of all their strength.
37. But bring out them with silver and with gold,
    Nor was there in their tribes one totterer.
38. Glad was Mizraim at their going forth,
    Because their dread had fallen upon them.
39. He spread a cloud to be a covering,
    Also a fire to be a light by night.
40. They asked, and then he would make quails come in,
    And bread of heaven he would sate them with.
41. He oped the rock, and waters would gush out,
    They flowed through arid places river-like.
42. And he did keep in mind his holy word,
    With Abraham who his own servant was;
43. And would bring forth his folk with joyfulness,

With gladsome singing his own chosen ones;
44. And he would give to them the heathens' lands,
And toil of other folks they shall possess,
45. In order that they might observe his statutes,
And that his law they carefully should keep.
O praise ye Jah!

PSALM CVI.

1.   O praise ye Jah!
Thank ye Jehovah, for that he is good;
For to eternity his mercy lasts.
2. Who can narrate Jehovah's mighty acts?
Can be proclaiming all the praise of him?
3. O happy they who judgement do observe,
He who at all times worketh righteously.
4.   Remember me, Jehovah,
      With favour of thy folk!
O visit me with thine own saving grace,
5. To see the welfare of thy chosen ones,
To gladden with thy nation's gladsomeness,
To glory with thine own inheritance.
6. We have been sinning with our forefathers,
We have been perverse, have done wickedly.
7. These forefathers of ours in Mizraim
Not wisely understood thy wondrous works,
Kept not in mind thy mercies multiplied,
But would rebel even at the sea of Suph.
8. Yet he would save them for his own name's sake,
Thereby to make his mightiness be known.
9. So when he chode the sea of Suph, it dried;
And he caused them to walk through surging deeps
      As if 'twere wilderness.
10. And he would save them from the hater's hand,

And would redeem them from the enemy's hand.
11. But waters covered their harassers up,
   Till not a single man of them was spared.
12. Then they would be believing in his words;
   They would be singing to the praise of him.
13. With reckless haste they did forget his works,
   They waited not upon his counselling:
14. But lusting wildly in the wilderness,
   Would tempt Almighty God in desert land.
15. So while he yielded to them what they asked,
   He also sent a leanness in their soul.
16. While they would grudge at Moses in the camp,
   At Aaron too, Jehovah's holy one,
17. The earth would gape, and swallow Dathan up,
   And cover o'er Abiram's company.
18. And fire would burn amid their company,
   A flame would set ablaze the wicked ones.
19. At Horeb they would fabricate a calf,
   And would do worship to a molten thing.
20. And they would change their proper gloriousness
   To statue of an ox that eateth grass.
21. They forgat God who had been saving them,
   The doer of great things in Mizraim,
22. Of wondrous things amid the land of Ham,
   Of fearful things beside the sea of Suph.
23. Then he would speak about destroying them,
   Unless that Moses, his own chosen one,
   Had stood within the breach before his face
   To turn his wrath back from destructiveness.
24. Then they refused the land of pleasantness;
   They did give no believing to his word:
25. But would be murmuring within their tents:
   They did not listen to Jehovah's voice.
26. So he was lifting up his hand at them,

To make them fall amid the wilderness,
27. And make their seed to fall 'mong heathen folks,
And to wide-scatter them throughout the lands.
28. Then they would join themselves to Baal-peor,
And eat the sacrifices of the dead;
29. And they would be provoking by their deeds,
So that a plague was breaking in on them.
30. Then would stand Phinehas, and interpose
In order that the plague might be restrained;
31. And this was put to him for righteousness
Through generations all for evermore.
32. Then they caused anger at font Meribah,
And ill did Moses fare because of them;
33. For they did irritate his spirit so
That he would speak out rashly with his lips.
34. They did not utterly destroy those folks
Regarding whom Jehovah spake to them;
35. But they would mingle with the nations round,
And they would learn the workings done by them.
36. And would subserve idolatries of them,
Till these became unto themselves a snare.
37. And they would sacrifice their very sons
And very daughters unto devilries;
38. And would pour out the blood of innocence,
The blood of sons and daughters of themselves,
In sacrifice to idols of Canaan;
So that the land became defiled with bloods.
39. And they would be polluting in their works,
And would be whoring in their own misdeeds.
40. Then glowed Jehovah's anger at his folk,
And he would loathe his own inheritance;
41. And he would give them into heathen hands,
So that their haters should rule over them;
42. And enemies should be oppressing them,

Until they be subdued beneath their hand.
43. Full many a time he would deliver them,
But they, they in their counsel would rebel,
And they fell low through their iniquity.
44. Yet he would see when they were in distress,
When he had hearing of their doleful cry.
45. And he would mind for them his covenant,
And would show pity in his mercy great.
46. And would procure for them compassioning
In presence of all those who captured them.
47. O save thou us, Jehovah our own God!
And gather us from 'mid the nations round,
To render thanks unto thy holy name,
And to be glorying in praise of thee.
48. Blest be Jehovah God of Israel,
Through all time past and through all time to come;
Also let all the people say, Amen.
O praise ye Jah!

PSALM CVII.

1. THANK ye Jehovah, for that he is good:
For to eternity his mercy lasts.
2. So let Jehovah's ransomed ones declare;
Those whom he ransomed from distressor's hand,
3. And out from lands he hath ingathered them,
From place of sunrise and from place of eve,
From north and from the sea.
4. Wandering in wilderness, in desert way,
A city of abode they did not find.
5. In hungriness as well as thirstiness,
Their soul within them would sink faintingly.
6. Then cry they to Jehovah in their plight,
And from their anguishments he'll rescue them,

7. And will direct them in a way straight on
   To go toward a city of abode.
8. O let them thank Jehovah for his mercy,
   And for his wonders to the sons of men!
9. For he hath satisfied the craving soul,
   The hungry soul too he hath filled with good.
10. Those dwelling amid darkness and death-shade,
    Bound in affliction and in iron chain,
11. Since they rebelled against the words of God,
    And the Most High One's counsel they contemned;
12. When he through trouble would subdue their heart,
    They stumbled down, and there was none to help.
13. Then cry they to Jehovah in their plight;
    Out from their anguishments he will them save,
14. Will bring them forth from darkness and death-shade,
    Also their bands he will asunder break.
15. O let them thank Jehovah for his mercy,
    And for his wonders to the sons of men!
16. For he hath shattered down the doors of brass,
    And he the bars of iron hath cut off.
17. Fools having through their course of trespassing,
    And through iniquities, run into grief,
18. All kinds of food they will in soul abhor,
    And will draw near the very gates of death.
19. Then cry they to Jehovah in their plight;
    Out from their anguishments he will them save,
20. Will send his word, and will be healing them,
    Will give escape from their corruptedness.
21. O let them thank Jehovah for his mercy,
    And for his wonders to the sons of men!
22. Yea, let them offer sacrifice of thanks,
    And celebrate his works in joyful song.
23. They who go down upon the sea in ships,
    Transacting business through the waters vast,

24. These men, yea, they have seen Jehovah's works
　　And wondrous doings in the shady deep,
25. 　　　　　When he would say,
　　And would be rousing a tempestuous wind,
　　　　Which would exalt his waves.
26. They'll go up heavens, they'll go down surge-deeps:
　　Their soul in evil case dissolves itself:
27. They reel and stagger like a drunken man,
　　And all their wisdom swallows itself up.
28. Then cry they to Jehovah in their plight,
　　And from their anguishments he'll bring them forth.
29. He'll still the tempest to a perfect calm,
　　And silent shall the billows be for them.
30. Then glad will they be that they are in quiet;
　　And he will lead them to the port they wish.
31. O let them thank Jehovah for his mercy,
　　And for his wonders to the sons of men!
32. Let them exalt him in the folk's assembly,
　　And in the elders' sitting give him praise!
33. He will set rivers to be wilderness;
　　And springs of water to be thirsty ground.
34. A land of fruit to be a place of salt,
　　For evilness of them who dwell therein.
35. He will set wilderness to water-pool,
　　And land of dryness to be water-springs;
36. And there he will cause hungry ones to dwell,
　　And they shall fix a city of abode;
37. 　　　　　And they will sow the fields,
　　　　　And they will plant the vines,
　　And shall work out the fruitage of increase.
38. When he will bless them, they shall much abound,
　　Also their cattle he will not make few.
39. When they shall become few, and bended down
　　Amid oppression, evilness, and grief,

40. He pouring out contempt on potentates,
    Will make these wander without aim or way;
41. But will bear high the needy one from harm,
    And will set families like flocks of sheep.
42. The upright ones beholding shall be glad,
    But all injustice shall have closed its mouth.
43. Whoso is wise and will observe these things,
    They shall perceive the mercies of Jehovah.

PSALM CVIII.

1. ESTABLISHT hath my heart been, O great God:
   I will be singing and attuning psalms;
      Yea, this my tongue shall do.
2. Do thou awake, O psaltery and harp,
      I shall awake the dawn.
3. I'll thank thee among peoples, O Jehovah;
   And will tune psalms of thee among the folks.
4. For great above the heavens thy mercy is;
   Also unto the skies hath been thy truth.
5. Be thou exalted above heavens, great God,
   And over all the earth thy gloriousness.
6. That thy beloved ones may be pulled through,
   O save with thy right hand, and answer me.
7. Great God hath spoken in his holiness;
   I will exult; I'll portion Shechem out;
   And Succoth's valley I will measure up.
8. Gilead is mine; Manasseh too is mine;
   And Ephraim is the stronghold of my head:
      Judah my lawgiver:
9.   Moab my washing-pan;
   Out over Edom I will cast my shoe,
   Over Philistia I will shout aloud.
10. Who will conduct me to the city fenced?

Who had upled me into Edom land?
11. Hast not, O God, thyself been spurning us?
And wilt not go, O God, before our hosts?
12. Vouchsafe to us a helping from distress,
For worthless is the saving help of man.
13. Through the great God we shall do valiantly;
And he, yea, he will tread our troublers down.

PSALM CIX.

1. GOD of my praise, do thou not heedless be!
2. Because a wicked mouth, and guileful mouth
   Against me they have oped,
They've spoke with me by tongue of falsity.
3. And they with words of hatred compassed me;
And they will fight against me without cause.
4. Flouting my love they treat me adversely;
   But I resort to prayer.
5.   And they will put on me
   Evil instead of good;
And hatred in requital of my love.
6. Do thou set over him a wicked man,
Also let Satan stand at his right hand.
7. When he is judged, let him go wicked thence;
His prayer too, let it be for a sin.
8. The days of him, let these be only few;
His overseership let another take.
9. His children, let them be in orphanhood,
   His wife in widowhood.
10. And let his children stroll in beggary
And in outseeking from their ruined wastes.
11. Let the extortioner trap all he hath;
And strangers plunder what his labour earns.
12. Let there be none to reach him mercy's aid;

And none to treat his orphans graciously.
13. Let his descendants be for cutting off;
In the next race outblotted be their name.
14.   Let there be kept in mind
The guilt of his forefathers to Jehovah,
Nor let his mother's sin be blotted out.
15. Be these before Jehovah constantly,
That he may cut from earth their memory.
16.   And for this very cause,
That he no mind had to be merciful;
But would pursue a man afflicted, needy,
And sore of heart, with an intent to kill.
17. He would love cursing, and it comes to him;
He had in blessing taken no delight,
    And it goes far from him.
18. He would be clothed with cursing as his robe,
And it goes in like water to his midst,
And like the oil into his very bones.
19. It shall be to him as his covering garb,
And for a belt he'll gird it constantly.
20.   Such recompense
Shall mine opposers from Jehovah get;
And those who do speak ill against my soul.
21. But O, do thou, Jehovah, Sovran Lord,
So deal with me as for thine own name's sake,
Since good thy mercy is, O rescue me!
22. For an afflicted needy one am I,
Also my heart is wounded in my midst.
23. Like shadow when it stretcheth I am gone,
I have been tost about like locust swarm.
24. My knees are faltering from abstinence,
Also my flesh hath failed of oiliness.
25. And I, I have been a reproach to them:
Whene'er they see me, they will shake their head.

26. Be helping me, Jehovah, O my God!
    O save thou me, as thou art merciful!
27. And they shall know that thine own hand is this;
    Thou, O Jehovah, thou hast wrought it out.
28.   Though cursing be those men,
           Yet thou, yea, thou wilt bless:
           They rose, but shall be shamed;
           Thy servant shall be glad.
29. Clothed with disgrace shall mine opposers be;
    And covered as in mantle with their shame.
30. I'll thank Jehovah greatly with my mouth,
    And in the midst of many I'll praise him.
31. For he will stand at needy one's right hand,
    To save from the condemners of his soul.

PSALM CX.

1. THUS hath Jehovah said unto my Lord,
           Sit thou at my right hand,
    Till I shall make thine enemies to be
           A stool beneath thy feet.
2.   The sceptre of thy strength
    Jehovah out from Zion will send forth:
    Do thou hold rule amid thine enemies.
3. Thy people willing in thy day of power,
    In holy beauties from the womb of dawn,
    Shall be to thee the dewing of thy youth.
4. Sworn hath Jehovah, and will not repent,
    That thou shalt be a priest for evermore
    After the order of Melchizedek.
5. The Sovran Lord at the right hand of thee
    Hath in his day of anger struck through kings.
6.   He will redress 'mong nations
           He hath filled up with bodies:

K

He hath struck through the head o'er earth's extent.
7. Out of a brook he in the way will drink;
Therefore he'll raise the head.

PSALM CXI.

1.   O praise ye Jah!
I'll thank Jehovah with whole-heartedness,
Where the upright and congregation meet.
2. Great have the workings of Jehovah been:
Sought out to the entire delight of them.
3. Grand and majestic hath his acting been,
Also his righteousness endures for aye.
4. He wrought memorial of his wondrous works:
Kind and compassionate Jehovah is.
5. A prey he gave unto his fearing ones,
He'll keep in mind for aye his covenant.
6. His power in working showed he to his folk,
By giving them the heathen's heritage.
7. The workings of his hands are true and just,
Reliable have all his precepts been.
8. Held firmly up for ever, evermore;
Wrought out are they in truth and uprightness.
9. Redemption he did send unto his folk;
He did ordain for aye his covenant.
Holy and reverend hath been his name.'
10. Wisdom's beginning is Jehovah's fear;
Behaviour good have all those doing them;
His praises shall endure for evermore.

PSALM CXII.

1.   O praise ye Jah!
O happy is the man who fears Jehovah,
In his commandment he hath great delight.

2. Mighty upon the earth shall be his seed;
   The race of upright people shall be blest.
3. Plenty and riches shall be in his house;
   Also his righteousness endures for aye.
4. There springs through darkness light for upright ones:
   Kind and compassionate and righteous man.
5. 'Tis well with him who showeth grace and lends;
   He will fulfil with judgement his affairs.
6. Surely for ever he shall not be moved;
   In long remembrance shall the righteous be.
7. From evil tidings he shall have no fear;
   Stablisht his heart is, trusting in Jehovah.
8. His heart held firmly up, he shall not fear.
   Till he shall see through those distressing him.
9. He hath dispersed, hath given to needy ones;
   His righteousness enduring evermore:
   His horn shall be upraised in gloriousness.
10. The wicked man shall see, and shall be vexed;
    His teeth he'll gnash, and he is melted off.
    Desires of wicked men shall perish quite.

PSALM CXIII.

1.   O praise ye Jah!
   Be giving praise, ye servants of Jehovah;
   Be giving praises to the name Jehovah.
2. O let the name Jehovah blessed be
   From present time and to eternity.
3. From rising of the sun to where it setteth
   Be praise abounding to the name Jehovah.
4. Raised high above all nations is Jehovah;
   Above the heavens is his gloriousness.
5. Who can be like Jehovah our own God?
   He who doth set himself high up to sit,

6. He who doth bend himself low down to see
    Throughout the heavens, and throughout the earth:
7. Who makes the wretched one rise up from dust;
    From dunghill he will raise the needy one,
8. That he may cause to sit along with chieftains,
        With chieftains of his folk;
9. Who makes the barren housewife to be sitting
        A mother glad with sons.
        O praise ye Jah!

PSALM CXIV.

1. When Israël came forth from Mizraim,
    The house of Jacob from a strange-tongued folk,
2. Then Judah did become his holy choice;
    And Israël was his dominion.
3. The sea beheld, and presently would flee;
    The Jordan would be turning itself back.
4. The mountains, they did skip about like rams,
    The little hills like younglings of the flock.
5. What aileth thee, O sea, that thou wilt flee?
    O Jordan, that thou wilt be turning back?
6. O mountains, that ye skip about like rams?
    O little hills, like younglings of the flock?
7. From presence of the Lord be pained, O earth;
    From presence of the God of Jacob's folk:
8. Who turns the rock into a water-pool,
    The very flint into a water-spring.

PSALM CXV.

1. Not unto us, Jehovah, not to us,
    But to thy name do thou give gloriousness,
    Upon thy mercy, and upon thy truth.

2. Why is it that the heathen nations say,
   Where, we would ask, can be the God of these?
3. While yet our God hath in the heavens been;
   Whate'er he took delight in he hath done.
4. Their idols are of silver and of gold,
   Which are the workings of the hands of men.
5. A mouth have these, but yet they cannot speak;
   Eyes they have got, but yet they cannot see;
6. Ears they have got, but yet they cannot hear;
   A nose they have, but yet they cannot smell.
7. The hands of them, but yet they cannot feel;
   The feet of them, but yet they cannot walk;
   They can give no expression through their throat.
8. Like unto them shall be those making them;
   Yea, every one who doth confide in them.
9. O Israel, confide thou in Jehovah:
   Their helper and their shielder he will be.
10. O house of Aaron, trust ye in Jehovah:
    Their helper and their shielder he will be.
11. Jehovah's fearers, trust ye in Jehovah:
    Their helper and their shielder he will be.
12. Jehovah hath remembered us; he'll bless;
    He will yet bless the house of Israël;
    He will yet bless the house of Aäron.
13. He will yet bless the fearers of Jehovah,
    Alike the little and the bigger ones.
14. Jehovah will be adding upon you,
    Upon yourselves, and also on your sons.
15. O blessed ye yourselves are of Jehovah,
    Who is the Maker of the heavens and earth.
16. The heavens, heavens for Jehovah are;
    But earth he giveth to the sons of men.
17. 'Tis not the dead who shall be praising Jah,
    Nor shall all they who down to silence go:

18. But we ourselves, we shall be blessing Jah,
    From present time and to eternity.
    O praise ye Jah!

PSALM CXVI.

1. I LOVE, because Jehovah listeneth
   Unto my voice, my supplicating cry.
2. Because he hath inclined his ear to me,
   I in my days will call.
3. Had gathered over me the cords of death,
   And straits of Sheol had been finding me;
   Distressfulness and sorrow I would find.
4. But in the name Jehovah I would call;
   O do, Jehovah, give my soul escape.
5. Gracious Jehovah is, and righteous too;
   Also our own God is compassionate.
6. Watchful o'er simple ones Jehovah is:
   I was brought low; but me he will make safe:
7. Return then, O my soul, unto thy rest,
   Because Jehovah hath dealt well to thee.
8. Since thou hast pulled away my soul from death,
   Mine eye from tearfulness,
   My foot from overthrow;
9. I shall walk on before Jehovah's face
   In lands of living men.
10. I have believed, therefore I will speak,
    I who was humbled much,
11. I who had said in mine affrighted haste,
    All mankind are untrue.
12. O what return shall I make to Jehovah
    For all his benefits bestowed on me?
13. The cup of full salvation I will lift,
    And on the name Jehovah I will call;

14. My vows unto Jehovah I will pay
   In presence, may it be, of all his folk.
15. O precious in Jehovah's sight shall be
   The death approaching to his saintly ones.
16.   Grant it, Jehovah, now,
       For I thy servant am;
   I am thy servant, son of thy handmaid:
       Thou hast unloosed my bonds.
17. To thee I'll offer sacrifice of thanks,
   And on the name Jehovah I will call:
18. My vows unto Jehovah I will pay
   In presence, may it be, of all his folk;
19. Within the precincts of Jehovah's house,
   Within the midst of thee, Jerusalem.
       O praise ye Jah!

PSALM CXVII.

1. Give praise unto Jehovah, all ye nations!
   Be ye applauding him, O all ye peoples!
2. For strong his mercy over us hath been,
   Jehovah's truth too shall endure for aye,
       O praise ye Jah!

PSALM CXVIII.

1. Thank ye Jehovah, for that he is good;
   For to eternity his mercy lasts.
2. O would that Israël were now to say,
   For to eternity his mercy lasts.
3. O that the house of Aaron now would say,
   For to eternity his mercy lasts.
4. O that Jehovah's fearers now would say,
   For to eternity his mercy lasts.
5. Out from the straits I called unto Jah,

And Jah hath answered me with ample room.
6. Jehovah for me, I shall have no fear;
What can be done to me by any man?
7. Jehovah's for me, with those helping me;
Therefore shall I see through those hating me.
8. 'Tis better to take shelter in Jehovah,
    Than to confide in man:
9. 'Tis better to take shelter in Jehovah,
    Than to confide in chiefs.
10. The nations all have been surrounding me;
But in Jehovah's name I'll mow them down.
11. Surrounding, yea, they've been surrounding me:
But in Jehovah's name I'll mow them down.
12.   Surrounding me like bees,
They have been quenched like as a fire of thorns,
And in Jehovah's name I'll mow them down.
13. Thrusting, thou hast been thrusting for my fall;
    Yet hath Jehovah helpèd me,
14.   My strength and song is Jah,
And he will be to me for saving help.
15. The voice of joyful singing and salvation
Shall be amid the tents of righteous men;
Jehovah's right hand doing valiantly.
16. Jehovah's right hand hath been raised aloft;
Jehovah's right hand doing valiantly.
17. I shall not die, but I shall be in life,
And I shall be declaring works of Jah.
18. Chastising, oft hath Jah chastisèd me,
But unto death he did not give me up.
19. Ope ye to me the gates of righteousness;
I'll enter through them, and be thanking Jah.
20. This then the gate unto Jehovah is;
The righteous ones shall enter in through it.
21. I will thank thee, for thou hast answered me.

And thou wilt be to me for saving help:
22. The very stone which builders did reject
Hath been promoted to the corner-head.
23. Forth from Jehovah this result hath come;
It is a doing wondrous in our eyes.
24. This is the day Jehovah hath wrought out;
We will rejoice and will be glad in it.
25. O pray, Jehovah, give salvation, pray!
O pray, Jehovah, cause to prosper, pray!
26. Blest he who cometh in Jehovah's name!
We wish you blessing from Jehovah's house.
27.   Almighty is Jehovah,
      And will give light to us.
O bind ye up the sacrifice with cords
Even unto the very altar horns.
28. My God art thou, and I will give thee thanks;
O thou my God, I will extol thee high.
29. Thank ye Jehovah, for that he is good;
For to eternity his mercy lasts.

PSALM CXIX.

1. O HAPPY those who perfect be of way;
Those who are walking in Jehovah's law.
2. O happy those who keep his testimonies;
With the whole heart they will be seeking him;
3. Yea, they have not been doing wrongfully;
    They in his ways have walked.
4. Thou hast commanded that precepts of thine
    Must be observed with care.
5. O that my ways should be establisht firm
    Thy statutes to observe.
6.   Then should I not be shamed
When looking closely to all thy commands.

7. I will thank thee in uprightness of heart
   When learning judgements of thy righteousness.
8. Thy statutes I will be observant of;
   Forsake me not unto extremity.

9. By what means shall a young man cleanse his path
   To an observance as befits thy word?
10. With my whole heart have I been seeking thee,
    Let me not wander off from thy commands.
11. Within my heart I have thy saying stored,
    On purpose that I may not sin to thee.
12. O blessed thou thyself Jehovah art;
    Teach me thy statutes well.
13. I with my lips have diligently told
    All judgements of thy mouth.
14. I in thy testimonies' way have joyed
    As o'er all plenteousness.
15. Upon thy precepts I will meditate,
    And I will fix my look upon thy paths.
16. I in thy statutes will delight myself;
    I shall not be forgetful of thy word.

17. Deal kindly to thy servant; I shall live,
    And I shall be observant of thy word.
18. Unveil mine eyes, and I will fix my look
    Upon the wondrous teachings of thy law.
19. A sojourner am I upon the earth,
    Do not be hiding from me thy commands.
20. My soul is strained in longing earnestness
    It hath toward thy judgements at all times.
21. Thou hast rebuked the proud accursed ones
    Who go a-wandering from thy commands.
22. Roll off from me reproaches and contempt,
    Because thy testimonies I have kept.
23. Though princes sat, and against me have talked,

Thy servant will upon thy statutes muse.
24. Thy testimonies too are my delights,
They are my counsellors.

25. My soul hath been down-clinging to the dust;
Keep me alive according to thy word.
26. My ways I've told, and thou wilt answer me;
Teach me thy statutes well.
27. Thy precepts' way cause me to understand,
And I will muse upon thy wondrous works.
28. My soul hath dropt because of heaviness;
Make me stand up according to thy word.
29. The way of falsity remove from me;
But thy love do thou grant me graciously.
30. The way of faithfulness hath been my choice;
Thy judgements I have fittingly esteemed.
31. I have been clinging to thy testimonies;
Jehovah, do thou not put me to shame.
32. The way of thy commandments I will run
When thou wilt give enlargement to my heart.

33. Point me, Jehovah, in thy statutes' way,
And I will closely keep it to the end.
34. Make me discern, and I'll close-keep thy law,
And will observe it with whole-heartedness.
35. Cause me to tread the path of thy commands,
For therein I delight.
36. Incline my heart unto thy testimonies,
And not to greed of gain.
37. Avert mine eyes from viewing vanity;
In thine own way do thou keep me alive.
38. Perform toward thy servant thine own saying,
Which tendeth to thy fear.
39. Avert thou my reproach, whereof I dread,
For thine own judgements have been very good.

40. Behold! I long toward precepts of thine;
    O in thy righteousness keep me alive.

41. And let thy mercies come to me, Jehovah;
    Thy saving help, as thou thyself hast said.
42. I'll answer my reproachers then a word;
    For I've confided in the word of thee.
43. And take not from my mouth the word of truth
        Unto extremity,
    For to thy judgements I have looked with hope.
44. And I'll observe thy law continually
        For ever and for aye.
45. And I shall walk about in ample room,
    Because thy precepts I have sought unto.
46. And I shall speak about thy testimonies
    In front of kings, and shall not be ashamed.
47. And I'll delight myself in thy commands,
        Which I regard with love;
48. And I'll lift up my palms to thy commands,
        Which I regard with love;
    And in thy statutes I will meditate.

49. Unto thy servant keep in mind the word
    Upon the which thou causedst me to hope.
50. This was my comfort 'mid my suffering,
    Because thy saying hath kept me alive.
51. Proud ones have scoffed at me excessively;
    From thine own law I have not turned aside.
52. I've kept in mind thy judgements of the past,
    Jehovah, and have comforted myself.
53. Horror intense hath taken hold on me,
    From wicked men abandoning thy law.
54. Sweet psalmings have thy statutes been for me
        In house of my sojourns.

55. By night I've kept in mind thy name, Jehovah,
    And I shall be observant of thy law.
56.   This hath been so to me
    Because thy precepts I have closely kept.

57. My portion, O Jehovah, I have said,
         Is to observe thy words.
58. I court thy presence with whole-heartedness;
    Show grace to me, as thou thyself hast said.
59. I have thought o'er my ways, and will anew
    Bring back my feet unto thy testimonies.
60. I've hasted, and without self-questioning
    To give observance unto thy commands.
61. The cords of wicked men have belted me;
    I of thy law have not forgetful been.
62. At midnight I will rise to give thee thanks,
    Upon the judgements of thy righteousness.
63. Fellow am I to all those fearing thee,
    And to observers of precepts of thine.
64. Jehovah, of thy mercy earth is full;
        Thy statutes teach thou me.

65. Good have thy dealings with thy servant been,
    Jehovah, in accordance with thy word.
66. Goodness of sense and knowledge teach thou me,
    Because in thy commands I have believed.
67. Ere I would answer I erred witlessly;
    But now thy saying I'm observant of.
68. O good art thou thyself, and doing good;
        Teach me thy statutes well.
69. Proud ones have forged against me falsity;
    I with whole heart will keep precepts of thine.
70. Insensible as fat hath been their heart;
    I in thy doctrine have had great delight.

71. 'Tis good for me that I had suffering,
   In order that thy statutes I should learn.
72. Better for me is doctrine of thy mouth
   Than thousands are of silver and of gold.

73. Thy hands have made me and will stablish me;
   O cause me to discern.
74. Those fearing thee shall see me, and be glad;
   For I toward thy word have looked with hope.
75.   Well know I, O Jehovah,
   That very righteousness thy judgements are,
   And faithfully thou hast afflicted me.
76. O let thy mercy for my comfort be,
   As thou thyself hast to thy servant said.
77. Let thy loves come to me, and I shall live,
   Because thy law hath been my great delight.
78. Shamed be the proud who falsely did me wrong;
   But I, yea, I will on thy precepts muse.
79. May there return to me those fearing thee,
   And those who do thy testimonies know.
80. Sound in thy statutes let my heart become,
   That I may not be shamed.

81. My soul hath languished for thy saving grace,
   Toward the word of thee I've looked with hope.
82. Mine eyes have languished for thy promises,
   So that I say, When wilt thou comfort me?
83. Though I have been like bottle amid smoke,
   Thy statutes I've not been forgetful of.
84. To what extent shall be thy servant's days?
   When wilt thou judge those persecuting me?
85. The proud ones have been digging for me pits,
   Which cannot be according to thy law.
86. All thy commandments have been faithfulness;

Falsely they persecute me; help thou me.
87. Almost they have consumed me in the land:
But I, thy precepts I do not forsake.
88. As fits thy mercy, O keep me alive;
And I'll observe the witness of thy mouth.

89.   For ever, O Jehovah,
The word of thee is stationed in the heavens.
90. From race to race thy faithfulness extends;
Thou didst establish earth, and it shall stand.
91. To thy appointments they have stood this day,
Because they all the servants are of thee.
92. Unless thy law had been my great delight,
Then I had perisht 'mid my suffering.
93. I nevermore thy precepts will forget,
Because through them hast thou kept me alive
94. To thee I do belong: O save thou me,
Because unto thy precepts I have sought.
95. For me wait wicked men to ruin me;
Thy testimonies I shall study well.
96. To all perfection I have seen an end,
But thy commandment is exceeding broad.

97. O what a love I bear unto thy law!
It is my meditation all the day.
98. Wise o'er my foes will thy commands make me,
Because for ever shall thy law be mine.
99. Better than all my teachers I am skilled,
For on thy testimonies I do muse.
100. More than old men I get to understand,
Because thy precepts I have closely kept.
101. From every evil path I've held my feet,
On purpose that I may observe thy word.
102. Off from thy judgements I do not depart

Since thou thyself hast been instructing me.
103. How sweet thy sayings to my palate! more
Than honey to my mouth.
104. I through thy precepts get to understand,
Therefore I hate whatever way is false.

105. A lamp unto my foot thy word hath been,
And light unto my path.
106. I have made oath, and I will stand to it,
Observing judgements of thy righteousness.
107. I have been suffering exceedingly:
Jehovah, quicken me, as saith thy word.
108. My mouth's free gifts do thou accept, Jehovah,
Also thy judgements do thou teach me well.
109. My soul is in my hand continually;
But of thy law I've not forgetful been.
110. The wicked men did lay a trap for me,
Yet from thy precepts I have wandered not.
111. I'll use thy testimonies evermore,
Because the joying of my heart are they.
112. I have inclined my heart for working out
Thy statutes to the furthest future end.

113. Unsteady thoughts I hate,
But thy law I do love.
114. My place of hiding and my shield art thou;
Toward the word of thee I've looked with hope.
115. Depart from me, ye evil-doing men,
And I will keep commandments of my God.
116. Uphold me as thou'st said, and I shall live;
And do not shame me from my eager hope.
117. Do thou sustain me, and I shall be saved,
And will respect thy statutes constantly.
118. Thou slightest all who from thy statutes err,

Because a falsity is their deceit.
119. Like dross thou quitt'st all wicked of the earth,
Therefore thy testimonies I have loved.
120. My flesh hath shuddered from a dread of thee;
And of thy judgements I have been afraid.

121. That which is just and righteous I have done;
O leave me not to my oppressive foes.
122. Be surety for thy servant unto good;
O let not proud ones be oppressing me.
123. Mine eyes do languish for thy saving grace,
And for the promise of thy righteousness.
124. Deal with thy servant as thy mercy prompts,
Also thy statutes do thou teach me well.
125. Servant of thee am I; make me discern,
And thus thy testimonies I shall know.
126. It is a time for working of Jehovah;
They have been making voidance of thy law.
127. Therefore have I loved thy commandments more
Than gold, and purest gold.
128. Therefore all precepts throughly I deem right,
But every path of falsity I hate.

129. O wonderful thy testimonies are!
Therefore my soul hath been close-keeping them.
130. The entrance of thy words will furnish light,
Inspiring simple minds.
131. My mouth I've set agape, and I will pant,
Because for thy commandments I have longed.
132. Turn thou toward me, and show grace to me,
As usual to them who love thy name.
133. My steps do thou establish in thy saying,
And let no godlessness have sway in me.

134. Redeem me from oppressiveness of man,
    And I shall then observe thy precepts well.
135. Thy face cause thou to shine upon thy servant,
    And be thou teaching me thy statutes well.
136. Streamlets of water from mine eyes run down
    Because they're not observant of thy law.

137. O truly righteous thou, Jehovah, art!
    Also straightforward have thy judgements been.
138. Thou didst command thy testimonies just,
    And faithful through and through.
139. My jealousy hath been suppressing me,
    Because my troublers have forgot thy words.
140. Thy saying is refined exceedingly,
    Also thy servant hath been loving it.
141. A little one am I, and am despised;
    Thy precepts I am not forgetful of.
142. Thy righteousness is righteous evermore,
    Also thy law is truth.
143. Distress and anguish have been finding me,
    Yet thy commandments are my great delight.
144. Righteous thy testimonies are for aye;
    Cause me to understand, and I shall live.

145. I've called with whole heart; do thou answer me;
    Jehovah, I thy statutes will close-keep.
146. I have called thee; O be thou saving me;
    And I thy testimonies will observe.
147. I foreran twilight, and would cry for help;
    Toward the word of thee I've looked with hope.
148. Mine eyes foreran the watches of the night,
    That I might muse upon thy promises.
149. My voice O hear thou, as thy mercy prompts,

As is thy wont, Jehovah, quicken me.
150. Near have come those who are on mischief bent:
Off from thy law they have been going far.
151. Full near hast thou thyself, Jehovah, been;
Also the whole of thy commands are truth.
152. Long have I from thy testimonies known
That thou for evermore hast founded them.

153. See thou my suffering, and pull me through,
Because thy law I'm not forgetful of.
154. Maintain my cause, and do thou ransom me,
To thine own promise do thou quicken me.
155. Far off from wicked men is saving grace,
For they unto thy statutes have not sought.
156. Many have thy compassions been, Jehovah;
As fits thy judgements do thou quicken me.
157. Many my chasers and my troublers are,
I from thy testimonies have not swerved.
158. I have seen traitors, and will loathing grieve
Because thy saying they have not observed.
159. O see thou that thy precepts I have loved;
Jehovah, in thy mercy quicken me.
160. The sum and substance of thy word is truth;
Also for evermore
Is every judgement of thy righteousness.

161. Princes have hunted me without a cause,
But from the word of thee my heart hath dread.
162. Joyful am I upon thy promises,
Like one who findeth an abundant spoil.
163. Falsehood I've hated, and I will abhor;
Thy doctrine I have loved.
164. Seven times a day I have been praising thee

Upon the judgements of thy righteousness.
165. Abundant peace have they who love thy law,
And unto them there is no stumblingblock.
166. I've eager looked for thy salvation, Lord,
And the commands of thee I have performed.
167. My soul thy testimonies hath observed,
And I will love them much.
168. I've been observant of thy preceptings
And of thy testimonies,
For all my ways have been in front of thee.

169. Let mine outcry go near thy presence, Lord,
According to thy word make me discern.
170. Let my beseeching go into thy presence;
As thou thyself hast said, O rescue me.
171. Freely my lips shall be outpouring praise
When thou'lt be teaching me thy statutes well.
172. My tongue shall to thy saying give reply,
For thy commandments all are righteousness.
173. O let thy hand be for a help to me,
Because thy precepts I have made my choice.
174. O I have longed for thy salvation, Lord;
Also thy law hath been my great delight.
175. O let my soul live, and be praising thee;
And let thy judgements give their help to me.
176. I have been wandering like sheep that's lost;
O seek thy servant out;
For thy commandments I have not forgot.

PSALM CXX.

1. Unto Jehovah in my growing straits
I have called out, and he will answer me.
2. Jehovah, be thou rescuing my soul

        From lip of falsity,
        From tongue of guilefulness.
3.   What will he give to thee,
        What will he add to thee,
        O tongue of guilefulness?
4. The sharpened arrows of a mighty man,
    Along with burning coals of juniper.
5. Woe's me! that I in Meshech have sojourned;
    That I have dwelt beside the Kedar tents.
6. Too long for its own good hath dwelt my soul
        With one who hateth peace;
7. I am most peaceful, but when I would speak,
        They are intent on war.

PSALM CXXI.

1. I WILL lift up mine eyes unto the hills;
    From whence is it that help shall come to me?
2. The help for me doth from Jehovah come,
    Who is the Maker of the heavens and earth.
3. May he not give removal to thy foot!
    May he not slumber who is keeping thee!
4. Behold! he will not slumber, nor will sleep,
        Who keepeth Israël.
5.   Jehovah keepeth thee;
        Jehovah is thy shade
        Upon right hand of thee.
6. By day the sun shall not be smiting thee,
        Nor shall the moon by night.
7. Jehovah will keep thee from every harm;
    He will be keeper of the soul of thee.
8. Jehovah, he will keep the going out
        And coming in of thee,
    From present time unto eternity.

PSALM CXXII.

1. Glad have I been with them who say to me,
   Let us be going to Jehovah's house.
2. Already standing have our feet been set
   Within the gates of thee, Jerusalem.
3. Jerusalem, which hath been builded up
   Like city which is well compact throughout;
4. To which go up the tribes, the tribes of Jah,
   A testimony unto Israël,
   To render thanks unto Jehovah's name.
5. For there the thrones of judgement have been set,
   The thrones for David's house.
6. Ask ye the welfare of Jerusalem;
   May those be prospered who are loving thee.
7. May there be peace within thy wall of strength;
   Prosperity within thy palaces.
8. For sake of mine own brethren and my friends,
   O let me speak, may there be peace in thee.
9. For home's sake of Jehovah our own God,
   I will seek good to thee.

PSALM CXXIII.

1. To thee have I been lifting up mine eyes,
   O thou who sittest in the heavens.
2. Behold! as turn the eyes of serving-men
   Toward the hand of their own masters;
   Or eyes of serving-maid
   Toward the hand of her own mistress;
   So will our eyes
   Be turned toward Jehovah our own God,
   Till he will show us grace.
3. Show grace to us, Jehovah; show us grace;

For much have we been sated with contempt.
4. Too much for it our soul hath sated been
With the derision of the self-secure,
With the contemning of the lordly proud.

PSALM CXXIV.

1. Unless Jehovah had been on our side,
O would that Israël were now to say;
2. Unless Jehovah had been on our side,
When up against us did mankind arise;
3. Then all alive they would have swallowed us,
When heated had their anger grown at us:
4. Then would the waters have o'erwhelmèd us;
The stream would have been passing o'er our soul:
5. Then would there have been passing o'er our soul
The waters in their haughty turbulence.
6.   Blest may Jehovah be,
Who hath not yielded us to be a prey
Unto the teeth of them.
7. Our soul like as a bird hath got escape
Out from the fowler's trap.
The trap is broken through;
And we, we verily, have got escape.
8. The help for us is in Jehovah's name,
The Maker of the heavens and the earth.

PSALM CXXV.

1. They who are trusting in Jehovah, these
Are like mount Zion; it shall not be moved;
For ever it shall sit.
2. Jerusalem hath hills surrounding her;
Also Jehovah is around his folk,
From present time, and to eternity.

3. For not shall rest the rod of wickedness
   On the allotment of the righteous ones;
   So that the righteous ones may not put forth
   Their hands to anything unjust.
4. Be doing good, Jehovah, to the good,
   Also to those straightforward in their hearts.
5. But those who turn aside their tortuous thoughts,
   Jehovah will cause them to go
   With workers of ungodliness.
   May peace be upon Israël.

PSALM CXXVI.

1. When Jehovah restored the abiding of Zion,
   Like dreamers were we.
2. Then was filling with laughter our mouth
   And our tongue with bright song.
   Then would they 'mong the heathen be saying,
   Great things hath Jehovah been doing with these.
3. Great things hath Jehovah been doing with us;
   And so we have been glad.
4. Yet restore, O Jehovah, our captives withdrawn
   Like the streams in the south.
5.   They who sow amid tears,
   Amid singing shall reap.
6. Though he go, though he go, and be weeping,
   While bearing some handfuls of seed;
   He shall come, he shall come with bright singing,
   While bearing his plentiful sheaves.

PSALM CXXVII.

1. Whene'er Jehovah would not build the house,
   In vain have any builders toiled at it.

    Whene'er Jehovah would not keep the town,
        In vain did keeper watch.
2. 'Tis vain for you at early hour to rise,
      At later hour to sit,
    Eating the bread of sore anxiety;
    Since he to his belov'd one will give sleep.
3.   Behold!
    Jehovah's own inheritance are sons;
    A recompense is fruitage of the womb.
4. Like arrows in the hand of warrior bold,
    Even so shall be the sons of youthfulness.
5.   O happy is the man,
    He who hath made his quiver full of them:
      They shall not be ashamed
    When they shall speak with foemen in the gate.

PSALM CXXVIII.

1. O HAPPY all who have Jehovah's fear,
      Each walker in the ways of him.
2. The labour of thy hands when thou shalt eat,
      O happy thou, and good for thee.
3. Thy wife shall be like to a fruitful vine
      Upon the sides of thine own house:
    Thy children shall be like to olive plants
      Surrounding thine own table-board.
4. Behold! how surely blest shall be the man
      Who hath Jehovah's fear!
5. Jehovah out from Zion will bless thee;
    And mayst thou see into Jerusalem's good
      Through all days of thy life.
6. Also mayst thou thy children's-children see.
    May peace be upon Israël.

PSALM CXXIX.

1. OFTTIMES have they harassed me from my youth;
    O would that Israel were now to say:
2. Ofttimes have they harassed me from my youth,
    Yet have not mastered me.
3. Upon my back the plowers have been plowing;
    They have made lengthy their afflictive scores.
4.   Jehovah righteous is;
    He cut in twain the cords of wicked men.
5. Ashamed shall be, and backward shall be turned,
    All who do Zion hate.
6. They shall be like the grass of the housetop,
    Which, ere it could unsheathe, has withered down;
7. With which no reaper ever filled his hand,
    No measurer his lap.
8. Nor hath been said by any passers-by,
    The blessing of Jehovah come to you;
    We give you blessing in Jehovah's name.

PSALM CXXX.

1.   OUT from the very depths
    I've called thee, O Jehovah.
2. Great Lord, do thou be listening to my voice;
    O let thine ears be turned attentively,
        While loud I supplicate.
3. Iniquities if thou wilt mark, O Jah,
        Great Lord, then who shall stand?
4. But yet with thee there is true pardoning
        That so thou mayst be feared.
5.   I've waited for Jehovah,
        Waiting hath been my soul;

And I toward his word have set my hope.
6.   My soul for the great Lord
Is waiting more than watchers for the morn
     A-watching for the morn.
7. Hope thou, O Israel, toward Jehovah;
For with Jehovah must true mercy be,
And plenteously with him redemption is.
8. And he, he is redeeming Israël
     From all iniquity.

PSALM CXXXI.

1. JEHOVAH, not high-set hath been my heart,
     Nor lofty were mine eyes;
Nor have I meddled among things too great,
Or among things too wonderful for me.
2.   I surely have well set
          And quieted my soul,
Like weaned child upon its mother's care;
Like weaned child upon me is my soul.
3. Hope thou, O Israel, toward Jehovah,
From present time and to eternity.

PSALM CXXXII.

1. REMEMBER, O Jehovah, David's case,
     With all his sufferings;
2. How he unto Jehovah did make oath,
He to the Mighty One of Jacob vowed:
3. I shall not go into the tent, my house;
I shall not go upon the couch, my bed;
4. I shall permit no sleeping for mine eyes
     Nor slumber for my lids,

5. Till I shall find a station for Jehovah,
   A dwelling-place for Jacob's Mighty One.
6. Behold! we heard of it in Ephratah;
   We found it in the fields of Ieärim.
7. Let us be going to his dwelling-place;
   Let us in worship at his footstool bow.
8. Arise, Jehovah, to thy place of rest!
   O thou thyself, and thine own ark of strength,
9. O let thy priests be clothed with righteousness:
   And let thy saints be shouting joyfully.
10. Even for David thine own servant's sake,
    O turn not thine anointed's face away.
11. Sworn hath Jehovah unto David truly;
    He'll not withdraw from it;
    Of thine own body's fruit
    I'll set on throne for thee.
12. If that thy sons observe my covenant
    And testimony which I'll teach to them;
    Likewise the sons of them through future time
    Shall sit on throne for thee.
13. Because Jehovah singled Zion out,
    Desired her for his seat;
14. This is my place of rest through future time;
    Here I will sit, for her I have desired.
15. Her sustenance with blessing I will bless;
    Her needy ones I'll satisfy with bread;
16. Also her priests I'll clothe with saving grace,
    Her saints shall sing, shall sing out joyfully.
17. There I will make a horn for David sprout;
    I've trimmed a lamp for mine anointed one.
18. The enemies of him I'll clothe with shame,
    But upon him shall flourish bright his crown.

PSALM CXXXIII.

1. Behold! O how good, and how pleasant
   The dwelling of brethren in union!
2. It is like the good oil on the head,
     Coming down on the beard,
     On the beard of Aharon;
   Which comes down on the mouth of his garments.
3.   Like the dewing of Hermon
   Which comes down on the mountains of Zion;
   For there hath Jehovah commanded the blessing,
     Even life everlasting.

PSALM CXXXIV.

1. Behold! be ye blessing Jehovah,
     All ye who are serving Jehovah,
   Who stand in the house of Jehovah by night,
2. By lifting your hands in devotion,
     And so be ye blessing Jehovah.
3. May blessing reach thee from Jehovah in Zion,
     The Maker of heaven and earth.

PSALM CXXXV.

1.   O praise ye Jah!
   Be giving praise unto the name Jehovah;
   Be giving praise, ye servants of Jehovah,
2. Ye who do stand within Jehovah's house,
   Within the courts of house of our own God.
3. Be praising Jah, for good Jehovah is;
   Attune ye to his name, for it is sweet.
4. For Jah hath chosen Jacob to himself;
   Israel to be his own dear property.

5. For I do know that great Jehovah is,
   And that our Lord is greater than all gods.
6. All things wherein Jehovah took delight
   He hath wrought out in heavens and on earth,
   Amid the seas, and all the surging deeps.
7. Making cloud-piles go up from end of earth;
   Bright lightning-bolts he for the rain hath made;
   Bringing the wind out from his storehouses.
8. He smote the eldest-born of Mizraim
           From mankind down to beast.
9. He did put forth his signs and miracles
   Into the midst of thee, O Mizraim,
   On Pharaoh and on all those serving him.
10. He smote the Gentile nations manifold,
    And slew the kings who were of mighty power:
11. As Sihon, who was king of Amorites,
    And Og, who was the king of Bashanites,
    And likewise all the kingdoms of Canaan;
12. And gave their lands to be a heritage,
    A heritage for Israël his folk.
13. Jehovah, thine own name shall be for aye;
    Jehovah, thy renown to ages all.
14. Because Jehovah will redress his folk,
    And to his servants will be pitiful.
15. The heathen idols silver are and gold;
    They are the working of the hands of man:
16. A mouth have they, but yet they cannot speak;
    Eyes they have got, but yet they cannot see;
17. Ears they have got, but they cannot give ear;
    Yea, there is not a breathing in their mouth.
18. Like unto these shall be those making them:
    Each one who doth put confidence in them.
19. O house of Israël, bless ye Jehovah!
    O house of Aharon, bless ye Jehovah!

20. O house of Levi, do ye bless Jehovah!
    Ye fearers of Jehovah, bless Jehovah!
21. O blessed be Jehovah out of Zion!
    Who dwelleth in Jerusalem,
        O praise ye Jah!

PSALM CXXXVI.

1. THANK ye Jehovah, for that he is good;
   For to eternity his mercy lasts.
2. O give ye thanks unto the God of gods,
   For to eternity his mercy lasts.
3. Give thanks unto the Sovran Lord of lords,
   For to eternity his mercy lasts.
4. To him who hath alone done wonders great,
   For to eternity his mercy lasts.
5. To him who made the heavens skilfully,
   For to eternity his mercy lasts.
6. To him who spread out earth above the floods,
   For to eternity his mercy lasts.
7. To him who was the Maker of great lights,
   For to eternity his mercy lasts.
8. Even the sun as ruler of the day,
   For to eternity his mercy lasts.
9. The moon and stars as rulers of the night,
   For to eternity his mercy lasts.
10. To him who smote all Mizraim's firstborn,
    For to eternity his mercy lasts.
11. And brought out Israël from midst of them,
    For to eternity his mercy lasts.
12. By a firm hand, and by a stretcht-out arm,
    For to eternity his mercy lasts.
13. To him who cut the sea of Suph in parts,
    For to eternity his mercy lasts.

14. And who made Israël cross through its midst,
    For to eternity his mercy lasts.
15. But shook off Pharaoh's force in sea of Suph,
    For to eternity his mercy lasts.
16. To him who marched his folk through wilderness,
    For to eternity his mercy lasts.
17. To him who was the smiter of great kings,
    For to eternity his mercy lasts.
18. And was the slayer of illustrious kings,
    For to eternity his mercy lasts.
19. As Sihon, who was king of Amorites,
    For to eternity his mercy lasts.
20. And Og, who was the king of Bashanites,
    For to eternity his mercy lasts.
21. And gave their lands to be a heritage,
    For to eternity his mercy lasts.
22. A heritage for Israël his servant,
    For to eternity his mercy lasts.
23. Who in our low estate remembered us,
    For to eternity his mercy lasts.
24. And he would snatch us from our harassers,
    For to eternity his mercy lasts.
25. The giver of provision to all flesh,
    For to eternity his mercy lasts.
26. Thanks do ye render to the God of heaven,
    For to eternity his mercy lasts.

PSALM CXXXVII.

1.   By the rivers of Babylon
   There we did sit, and moreover did weep
      While remembering Zion.
2.   Upon willows in midst of her
   We had been hanging our harps.

3. But there did our captors claim for us
    The words of a song;
    And our spoilers claimed gladness;
  Come, sing us a lyric of Zion.
4. How can we sing songs of Jehovah
    On the soil of a stranger?
5. If I forget thee, O Jerusalem,
    Then let my right hand forget.
6. Let be clinging my tongue to my palate,
    If fails my remembrance of thee;
    If I bring not Jerusalem up
    On the top of my gladness.
7. Remember, Jehovah, against Edom's sons
    That Jerusalem day,
  When they said, Make ye bare, make her bare
    To the very foundation.
8. O daughter of Babel, thou doomed one!
  Happy he who shall pay back to thee
  The same treatment thou gavest to us!
9. Happy he who shall seize, and shall dash
  Thy young children against the stone crag!

PSALM CXXXVIII.

1. I will thank thee with all my heart.
  Before the gods I will attune of thee.
2. I will bow down toward thy holy temple,
    And I will thank the name of thee,
  Upon thy mercy, and upon thy truth:
  For thou hast magnified o'er all thy name
    Thy promises.
3. What day I called, then thou wouldst answer me;
  Thou wouldst inspire me in my soul with strength.
4. Thank thee, Jehovah, shall all kings of earth,

When they have heard the sayings of thy mouth,
5. And they will sing along Jehovah's ways,
For great the glory of Jehovah is.
6. Though high Jehovah, yet the low he'll see,
Also the proud ones from afar he'll know.
7. Though I should walk amid distressfulness,
Thou wilt keep me alive;
On my foes' anger thou wilt send thy hand,
But thine own right hand shall be saving me.
8. Jehovah will complete concerning me;
Jehovah, since thy mercy lasts for aye,
Leave not the works of thine own hand to fail.

PSALM CXXXIX.

1. JEHOVAH, thou hast searched me, and wilt know:
2. Thou, thou hast known my sitting and my rising:
Hast understood my inner thoughts from far.
3. My going and my lying thou dost sift,
And all my ways thou art acquainted with.
4. Though there be not a word upon my tongue,
Lo! thou, Jehovah, hast known all of it.
5. Behind, before, thou hast beleaguered me,
And thou wilt lay on me thine open hand.
6. Too wonderful this knowledge is for me;
Set up so high, I cannot reach to it.
7. O whither can I from thy Spirit go?
Or whither from thy presence shall I flee?
8. If I should mount the heavens, there art thou!
Or make my couch in Sheol, behold thee!
9. Were I to lift the wings of morning dawn;
Were I to dwell in utmost end of sea;
10. There also would thy hand be leading me,
And holding me would be thine own right hand.

11. I might say, Ah! the dark will smother me;
    Then hath the night been light surrounding me.
12. Even the darkness darkeneth not from thee;
    But night like as the day will furnish light,
    Alike the darkness and the brightness are.
13. Since thou, thou wast possessor of my reins,
    Thou wouldst o'ershade me in my mother's womb,
14. I'll thank thee for my fearful wondrousness;
    O wondrous are thy works!
    Also my soul is knowing this right well.
15. Not hidden was my body-frame from thee
    When I was being made in secret place,
    Embroidered in the lower parts of earth.
16. My growing embryo thine eyes have seen,
    And on thy book would all of them be writ,
    The days that they were formed,
    While none of them yet was.
17. And toward me how precious are thy thoughts,
    O God, how great have been the sums of them!
18. I would recount them, they outnumber sand:
    I have awaked; and still I am with thee.
19. If thou wilt kill, O God, the wicked man,
    Then, O ye men of blood, depart from me:
20. Those who while naming thee for ill device
    Have acted impiously, as foes of thee.
21. Thy haters, O Jehovah, shan't I hate?
    At thy withstanders shan't I loathing grieve?
22. With perfect hatred I have hated them;
    As enemies they have become to me.
23. Make search of me, O God, and know my heart;
    Be trying me, and know my flitting thoughts:
24. And see if there be grievous way in me;
    And lead me in the everlasting way.

PSALM CXL.

1. OUTRID me, O Jehovah, from ill men!
   From men of violence preserve thou me!
2. Those who have plotted evil things in heart;
   Who all the day are mustering for wars.
3. They've made their tongue sharp-pointed, serpent-like;
   An adder's poison is beneath their lips.   Selah.
4. Keep me, Jehovah, from the wicked's hands;
   From man of violence preserve thou me;
   Those who have plotted to thrust down my steps.
5. The proud have hid a trap for me, and cords;
   They have spread out a net beside the track;
       Snares they have laid for me.   Selah.
6. I've to Jehovah said, My God art thou;
   Hear, O Jehovah, my beseeching voice.
7. Jehovah Lord, thou my salvation's strength,
   Wast shielding o'er my head in battle-day.
8. Grant not, Jehovah, wicked man's desires;
   His plots succeed not; they would be elate.   Selah.
9.   The head of those around me,
   Their own lips' grievousness shall cover them.
10. Moved down upon them shall be burning coals;
        In fire he'll make them fall;
    Into deep sloughs from which they shall not rise.
11. A man of tongue shall not thrive in the land;
        A man of violence,
    Evil shall hunt him to a speedy fall.
12. Well know I that Jehovah will work out
    The sufferer's redress, the needy's due.
13. Ah! men of righteousness will thank thy name:
    The upright ones shall in thy presence sit.

PSALM CXLI.

1. Jehovah, I have called thee; haste to me;
   O hear my voice when I do call to thee.
2. Accept my prayer as incense before thee;
   My lifted hands as evening offering.
3. Set thou, Jehovah, to my mouth a watch,
   A guard upon the doorway of my lips.
4. Let not my heart incline to evil word,
   To practise practisings of wickedness,
   Along with men who work ungodliness:
   Nor let me feed in their festivities.
5. A righteous man might strike me; that were kind:
   Or might reprove me; that were oil on head:
   Nor should my head refuse it, though prolonged.
   But I would pray 'mid their injuriousness.
6. Their judges were let off beside the crag;
   And they did hear my sayings, which were sweet.
7. As when one cuts and cleaves upon the land,
   Our bones were scattered about Sheol's mouth.
8. Yet toward thee, Jehovah, Sovran Lord,
   Mine eyes are set; in thee I'm sheltering:
   O make not bare my soul!
9. Keep me from hands of trap they've laid for me,
   And snares of workers of ungodliness.
10. Fall down in their own nets shall wicked men;
    While I myself shall pass entirely by.

PSALM CXLII.

1. Aloud I to Jehovah will cry out;
   Aloud I to Jehovah will beseech.
2. I will pour out before him my complaint;
   My trouble I before him will display.

3. When sinking faint within me was my spirit,
Then thou, yea, thou hadst knowledge of my course;
In that same path wherein I use to go,
    They've hid a trap for me.
4. Be looking to the right hand, and see thou
    That I have no acknowledger,
    That refuge hath quite failed from me.
    That none is caring for my soul.
5. I have cried out, Jehovah, unto thee;
I have been saying, Thou my shelter art,
My portion in the land of living men.
6. Do thou be giving heed to mine outcry,
    For I'm brought very low.
O rescue me from those pursuing me,
    For they're too strong for me.
7. Do thou bring out from prison-house my soul,
    To thanking of thy name.
Around me will the righteous congregate
    When thou wilt kindly deal to me.

PSALM CXLIII.

1. JEHOVAH, be thou listening my prayer;
Do thou give ear unto my supplications:
O in thy faithfulness do answer me
    In thine own righteousness.
2. And come not into judgement with thy servant,
For before thee none living can be righteous.
3. Because the enemy pursues my soul,
He hath been crushing to the earth my life;
He hath caused me to sit in darknesses
    Like dead men of the past.
4. And sinking is my spirit faint in me;
In midst of me my heart is desolate.

5. I've called to memory the days of old,
   Have meditated upon all thine acts:
   Upon the working of thy hands I'll muse.
6. I have been spreading out my hands to thee,
   My soul like as a weary land to thee.   Selah.
7. O do thou haste to answer me, Jehovah!
         My spirit languisheth:
   Do not be keeping hid thy face from me,
   Lest I be classed with goers-down to pit.
8. Cause me to hear at morning-time thy mercy,
         For I in thee confide:
   Cause me to know the way that I should walk,
   For unto thee have I lift up my soul.
9. Me rescue from mine enemies, Jehovah;
         With thee I've cover sought.
10. Do thou teach me to do what pleaseth thee,
         Because thou art my God:
    Let thy good Spirit be conducting me
         In land of levelness.
11. Even for sake of thine own name, Jehovah,
         Thou wilt keep me alive;
         In thine own righteousness
    Thou wilt bring forth out of distress my soul.
12.   And thou in mercy wilt
         Suppress mine enemies;
    And hast destroyed all who harass my soul;
         For I thy servant am.

PSALM CXLIV.

1. O BLESSED be Jehovah, my strong rock!
   Who is the trainer of my hands for war,
   And of my fingers for the battle's brunt:
2.   My mercy and my fortalice,

My safe high-place, and my deliverer;
My shield, and in him I have shelter found;
Subduer of my people under me.
3.　　　　　　Jehovah,
O what is man, that thou wilt know of him?
Frail son of man, that thou wilt think of him?
4. Man who to very vanity is like;
His days are as a shadow passing by.
5. Jehovah, bow thy heavens, and come down;
Touch thou the mountains so that they shall smoke;
6. Enlighten lightning, and forth scatter them;
Send out thine arrows, and discomfit them.
7. Send out thy hands from the exalted height;
Do thou be snatching me and rescuing me
　　　From waters manifold,
　　　From hand of stranger sons:
8. Those men whose mouths have spoken worthlessness,
And whose right hand is hand of falsity.
9. Great God, a new song I will sing to thee;
On ten-stringed psaltery I'll tune to thee;
10. The giver of salvation to the kings;
The snatcher of his servant David free
　　　From the injurious sword.
11. Do thou be snatching me, and rescuing me
　　　From hand of stranger sons;
Those men whose mouths have spoken worthlessness,
And whose right hand is hand of falsity.
12. But let the sons of us be like to plants
Grown vigorously in their youthfulness;
Our daughters, may they be like cabinets
Carved in the style of temple ornaments.
13. Our storehouses, may they be amply full,
Affording their supplies from kind to kind:
Our flocks, may they be bearing thousandfold,

　　　　　Till they be myriads on our open lands:
14. Our carrier-cattle busy at their load;
　　　No breaking in, nor any going forth;
　　　And no complaining cry upon our streets.
15. Happy the folk who have it thus with them:
　　　Happy the folk whose God Jehovah is.

PSALM CXLV.

1. I WILL extol thee, O my God, the King:
　　　And I will bless thy name for evermore.
2. Through every day I will be blessing thee,
　　　And I will praise thy name for evermore.
3. Great is Jehovah, and supremely praised,
　　　And of his greatness there can be no search.
4. Race unto race shall celebrate thy works,
　　　Also thy mighty deeds they shall display.
5. The glorious honour of thy majesty,
　　　And matters of thy wondrous works I'll muse.
6. The powerfulness of thy dread acts they'll tell;
　　　And of thy greatnesses I'll make recount.
7. In mind of thy much goodness they'll talk oft,
　　　And of thy righteousness they'll brightly sing.
8. Kind and compassionate Jehovah is;
　　　To anger slow, in mercy he is great.
9. Good is Jehovah unto everything;
　　　And his compassion is o'er all his works.
10. Thank thee, Jehovah, shall thy works each one;
　　　Also thy saints, they will be blessing thee.
11. The glory of thy kingdom they will tell,
　　　And of thy mightiness they will speak forth.
12. 　　　　　That so may be made known
　　　Unto the sons of men his mighty deeds,
　　　And glory of his kingdom's majesty.

13. Thy kingdom is a kingdom everlasting,
    Thy rule too is through generations all.
14. A stay Jehovah is for all who're falling;
    A lifter up for all who are bowed down.
15. The eyes of all to thee will eager wait,
    And thou dost give to them
    Their food in season due.
16. Thou openest thy hand,
    And satisfiest every creature's want.
17. Righteous Jehovah is in all his ways,
    And merciful is he in all his works.
18. Near is Jehovah to all calling him,
    To all who will be calling him in truth.
19. The pleasure of his fearers he will do;
    Their cry for help he'll hear, and will them save.'
20. Jehovah keepeth all his loving ones,
    But all the wicked ones he will destroy.
21. Praise of Jehovah let my mouth speak out;
    And may all flesh bless holy name of him
    For ever, evermore.

PSALM CXLVI.

1. O praise ye Jah!
   Give praise unto Jehovah, O my soul.
2. I'll give Jehovah praises while I live;
   I'll tune to my God while my being lasts.
3. Put not your confidence in princely men,
   In son of man who hath no saving power.
4. Forth goes his breath; he to his soil returns;
   In that same day his busy thoughts are lost.
5. Happy whoe'er hath Jacob's God for help;
   Who waiteth on Jehovah his own God:
6. The Maker of the heavens and the earth,

With sea, and with whatever is in them;
Observer of the truth for evermore:
7. Who doeth judgement for oppressed ones;
Who giveth bread unto the famisht ones;
Jehovah looseth the imprisoned ones;
8. Jehovah openeth the blinded eyes;
Jehovah straightens up the bowed down;
Jehovah loveth men of righteousness.
9. Jehovah watcheth over sojourners;
The orphan and the widow he will aid;
But ways of wicked men he will subvert.
10. Reign shall Jehovah to eternity:
Thy God, O Zion, through each future race.
O praise ye Jah!

PSALM CXLVII.

1. O be ye praising Jah, for it is good;
Attune thou of our God, for it is sweet;
A comely thing is praise.
2. Jerusalem's upbuilder was Jehovah;
Outcasts of Israël he'll gather in.
3. 'Tis he who healeth those of broken heart,
And is the binder of their painful wounds.
4. He counteth up the number of the stars;
To every one of them he calls by name.
5. Great is our Lord, and of abounding strength;
His understanding is beyond account.
6. The aider of the meek Jehovah is;
The humbler down of wicked ones to earth.
7. Give answer to Jehovah with your thanks;
Attune ye to our own God with a harp.
8. 'Tis he who covereth the heavens with clouds;
Who doth establish for the earth its rain;

Who causeth mountains to put forth their grass.
9. He giveth to the quadruped its food;
To sons of ravens when they're calling out.
10. Not in the might of horse will he delight;
Nor in the legs of man will he be pleased.
11. Pleased is Jehovah with those fearing him,
With those who to his mercy look in hope.
12. Laud thou Jehovah, O Jerusalem!
Be giving praise, O Zion, to thy God!
13. For he made firm the barrings of thy gates;
He blessed thy children in the midst of thee.
14. 'Tis he who setting on thy border peace,
With fat of wheat will be sufficing thee.
15. 'Tis he who sends his saying o'er the earth,
So that right speedily his word shall run.
16. 'Tis he who giveth snow as it were wool;
Hoar-frost like as fine ash he scattereth.
17. He casteth forth his ice like brittle cakes;
In presence of his freezing who may stand?
18. He will send forth his word, and make them melt:
His wind shall blow, and then the waters flow.
19. He showeth his own word to Jacob's folk,
His statutes, judgements unto Israël.
20. Not so to every nation hath he done;
And judgements, these they have not known at all.
O praise ye Jah!

PSALM CXLVIII.

1.   O PRAISE ye Jah!
Give praise unto Jehovah from the heavens;
Give praise to him in the exalted heights:
2. Give praise to him, O ye his angels all;
Give praise to him, O all ye hosts of his;

3. Give praise to him, O ye both sun and moon;
   Give praise to him, O all ye stars of light:
4. Give praise to him, ye heavens of the heavens;
   Also ye waters which be o'er the heavens;
5. Let them give praise unto Jehovah's name;
   At whose commandment they created were;
6. And who will make them stand for evermore:
   Decree he gave, and it shall not pass off.
7. Give praise unto Jehovah from the earth,
   Ye monster creatures, and all surging deeps,
8. Both fire and hail, both snow and vap'rous smoke;
   Thou wind of tempest, working out his word;
9. Both ye the mountains, and all little hills;
   Fruit-bearing wood, and every cedar-tree:
10. Ye animals, and all the cattle kind;
    The creeping creatures, and the winged bird;
11. The kings of earth, and peoples every one;
    Princes, and all the judges of the earth:
12. Ye choice of manhood, and ye virgins too;
    Ye aged men, along with juveniles:
13. Let them give praise unto Jehovah's name;
    For set on high is name of him alone:
    His splendour is upon the earth and heavens.
14. And he'll exalt a horn for his own folk,
    A theme of praise for all his sainted ones,
    For Israel's sons, a people near to him.
        O praise ye Jah!

PSALM CXLIX.

1.   O PRAISE ye Jah!
   O sing ye to Jehovah a new song!
   His praise in congregation of the saints.
2. O glad may Israel be in his Maker;

Let sons of Zion triumph in their King.
3. O let them praise the name of him in dance:
Timbrel and harp let them attune to him.
4. For pleased Jehovah is with his own folk;
He'll beautify the meek with saving grace.
5. O let the saints exult in gloriousness,
Let them be brightly singing on their beds.
6. The Almighty's lofty praises in their throat;
Also a two-edged sword within their hand,
7. For working out of vengeance on the nations,
Of chastisements upon the heathen folks;
8. For binding up the kings of them with chains,
Their men of mark with iron fetterings:
9. For working on them the forewritten doom:
An honour this for all his sainted ones.
O praise ye Jah!

PSALM CL.

1. O PRAISE ye Jah!
O praise ye God in his own holiness!
O praise him in the outspread of his power!
2. Be praising him in his almighty deeds;
Be praising him so manifoldly great;
3. Be praising him with blowing of the horn;
Be praising him with psaltery and harp;
4. Be praising him with timbrelling and dance;
Be praising him with minnim and with flute;
5. Be praising him with cymbals of loud sound;
Be praising him with cymbals' joyful clang.
6. Let universal breath be praising Jah;
O praise ye Jah!

www.ingramcontent.com/pod-product-compliance
Lightning Source LLC
Chambersburg PA
CBHW032134160426
43197CB00008B/635